.........THE BEST IS FOR US TO MAKE.........

烹飪精華

周蘭香著

EXCEL IN CHINESE COOKING

WITH
LONNIE MOCK

ALPHA GAMMA ARTS
WALNUT CREEK, CALIFORNIA
1982

ALPHA GAMMA ARTS
P. O. BOX 4671
WALNUT CREEK, CALIFORNIA 94596-0671

ISBN 0-941716-00-7

LIBRARY OF CONGRESS CATALOG CARD NUMBER 81-70318

PRINTED IN THE UNITED STATES OF AMERICA
FIRST EDITION

IN PURSUIT OF

E L E G A N C E ,
P E R F E C T I O N
&
E X C E L L E N C E

FOREWORD

It is an honor for me to be asked to write this foreword by my friend, Lonnie Mock. This is a truly creative cookbook to give you self-confidence to prepare fabulous Chinese dishes as well as to experience marvelous dining pleasure.

Her recipes have all been tested over and over for easy to read usage, for easy to secure ingredients, for easy to prepare methods and above all to yield easy to enjoy creations!

Lonnie was born in Hong Kong and spent her early childhood in Macao. She majored in mathematics and education at San Diego State University and at the University of California, Berkeley.

She presently teaches mathematics at Diablo Valley College and instructs her real love, Chinese cooking, in Bay Area classes. Miraculously she also conducts a cooking program on educational television on occasion. One of her favorite hobbies is gardening and preserving the fruits of the Earth.

She credits her mother with her first lessons in Chinese cuisine. From there she has adapted recipes for practical application so that exciting real Chinese meals can be duplicated in your own American kitchen.

As a former cooking teacher and an active author of Chinese and Japanese cookbooks myself I can highly recommend EXCEL IN CHINESE COOKING for beginners and gourmet cooks alike.

The imaginative, exciting, very detailed index of this book will encourage you to try every unusual recipe--Honey Jerky, Mongolian Beef, Stuffed Boneless Whole Duck, Three-

Flavored Prawns, Sesame-Peanut Soup, Won Ton War Mein, etc.....the sparkling titles alone make your salivary glands flow!!!

Try also Lonnie's other publications: FAVORITE DIM SUM and 141 AND ONE-HALF CHINESE-STYLE CHICKEN RECIPES. They are all excellent additions to your cookbook library. Great adventure is ahead for you within the pages to follow. ENJOY!

Kay Shimizu
Author of Asian Cookbooks

Saratoga, California
November, 1981

INTRODUCTION

EXCEL IN CHINESE COOKING is another offshoot of my love for cooking. It is the fruit of five years of teaching. Continuous inquiries, encouragement and compliments from students and fans afar have resulted in the present work. This book provides a perfect balance for FAVORITE DIM SUM, of which 141 AND ONE-HALF CHINESE-STYLE CHICKEN RECIPES is an offshoot. EXCEL IN CHINESE COOKING covers a wide range of dishes--beef, pork, poultry, seafood, vegetables, noodles and rice, and dim sum, whereas the other cookbooks represent specialties as indicated by their titles. All three volumes complement each other.

It has been said, "Where there is smoke, there is Chinese". To this, I would add "and a Chinese restaurant". While this statement may be an exaggeration, it is a fact that Chinese restaurants and cooking schools are being established in most major cities of the world. It seems as if a culinary revolution is taking place. People everywhere have discovered the wonders and healthy ways of Chinese cooking. Homecooked Chinese meals, indeed, are generally economical, low in calories, and are well-balanced delicious meals. Stir-fried vegetables, for example, retain their natural nutrients, brilliant color and texture. And because food cooks so rapidly, fuel is conserved.

Dim sum, defined as "Chinese snacks" in Chinese dictionaries, is also poetically defined as "heart's delight". Dim sum has become popular in recent years. Flourishing teahouses indicate that this popularity will continue to grow. Dim sum dishes are commonly served for tea lunch, but a great number of dim sum morsels can be served as party hors d'oeuvres, an ideal food for perfect and elegant entertaining. Do not be intimidated by the length of some of these recipes. They may seem complicated but they certainly are not hard to do. Dim sum making is no more difficult than pie baking. Perhaps the "difficulty" lies in unfamiliarity. Anticipating this, I have included close-up photos of these delectables and step-by-step illustrations to lead you to success. Preliminary preparations can be done in advance and dumpling forming can be shared by family members and friends. It is also a fun way to introduce youngsters to the joy of cooking. Dim sum making is an art, an art that can be easily mastered by practice.

Included in this collection are fancy garnishes, a fascinating art by itself. Garnish adds eye appeal, may it be gourmet or simple fare. It transforms the ordinary into the elegant. Best of all, garnishes are easy to make and can be done leisurely. Invited to dinner, a friend once remarked she felt that her hostess loved her dearly because every dish was prepared and decorated with tender loving care. In this respect, beautiful garnish reflects warmth and cordial reception.

EXCEL IN CHINESE COOKING is an accumulation of recipes I have formulated based on authentic Chinese culinary tradition; and if there is any adaptation or substitution, it was done without the sacrifice of good flavor. This does not mean that all recipes call for exotic ingredients or a special trip to Chinatown. On the contrary, most ingredients are conveniently obtainable at local supermarkets. Chinese are adaptive and creative, and cook with whatever is readily available yet still achieve a delightful dish that is distinctively Chinese. While a small number of recipes require perfect timing and lengthy preparation, the majority of the recipes can be prepared in a relatively short period of time. Much of the preparation, lengthy or not, can be done beforehand.

This volume is composed of 181 recipes with manifold variations. By using a different seasoning or applying a different cooking technique, the dish will instantly take on a new delightful flavor. These recipes strive to bring out scrumptious gourmet specialties, low-calorie favorites, dazzling desserts and everyday fare, providing a large selection for experienced cooks as well as beginners. Some recipes yield savory Cantonese-style dishes, some are spicy, and some are combinations of the best from different regions.

EXCEL IN CHINESE COOKING is a friend--a friend who holds you by the hand and guides you to take a few giant steps forward in this enormous world of Chinese cuisine. Follow directions--at least for the first time--have patience, be persistent, use a little imagination and aim to achieve the utmost. In other words, experiment whole-heartedly with enthusiasm to become an accomplished cook. Why pursue excellence? There is an old Chinese proverb: "Eat the best!"

My ultimate goal is to give dependable recipes with precise directions so the family chef can expand his or her cooking techniques and skills and create mouth-watering Chinese meals at home. For beginners, perhaps it is best to start with the simpler recipes. Once you have absorbed the basic knowledge, curiosity and challenge will lead you to approach the more complicated or unfamiliar recipes with confidence.

I cordially invite you to join this culinary revolution, experience the art and joy of Chinese cooking, and excel.

Lonnie Mock

ACKNOWLEDGMENT

MY SINCERE AND HEARTFELT THANKS TO KAY SHIMIZU WHOSE SUPPORT HAS BEEN
IMMEASURABLE, TO NANCY HAGGERTY WHO LABORED WITH DEVOTION IN EDITING,
TO ROSE NEL KAUDER WHO CAREFULLY AND PATIENTLY PROOF READ THE TEXT;
AND SPECIAL GRATITUDE TO JEFF, WHO BELIEVES IN MY ENDEAVOR.

CONTENTS

SWEET TAMALES, page 137

GIN DOY, page 181

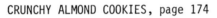

CRUNCHY ALMOND COOKIES, page 174

MINI SPONGE CAKE, page 183

Chop. Cut into pieces of any shape.

Crush. Pound with flat surface of cleaver or use crusher.

Cube. Cut into 1/2", 3/4" or desired chunks.

Dice. Cut into pea-sized cubes.

Matchstick-cut. Cut into long narrow thin strips resembling matchsticks.

Mince. Chop finely.

Score. Diagonally cut in crisscross pattern. Do not cut through. This helps to tenderize the meat.

Shred. Cut with grain into long strips. Slice strips against grain or diagonally, then cut slices into fine strips. Shred root vegetables with shredder if used for filling.

Slice. Cut with grain into long strips, then cut thinly against grain or diagonally.

Sliver. Cut into narrow thin strips similar to matchstick-cut but finer and shorter.

PAN-FRIED TURNIP CAKES, page 159

SAUSAGE TURNIP CAKE, page 158

Our goal is to bone the whole fowl without cutting it into parts or rearranging the body in any way. Remove excess fat from cavity and neck, pluck pinfeathers, and clean inside and outside of bird. Starting from the neck, separate meat from the wishbone by cutting close to the bone along the "V". Run a thumb between the breast meat and center breast bone to free the meat from bones as far down as you can. Next, disjoint a drummette from the shoulder (cut from the inside of neck cavity). Cut meat around the drummette bone, pushing the meat with skin downward as you cut. Cut off the drummette bone at the second joint of the wing. (The wing tip and middle section of the wing still have their bones left in.) Do the same with the other drummette. From here on down, it is easy. Pull the breast meat with skin down to the thighs, then pull the skin with meat off the back down to the thighs also. Disjoint thigh bones from body and cut tail off so that it is attached to the skin. Pull the carcass bone away. Now the whole carcass bone is all out and in one piece. Finally, debone the legs by cutting the meat from the thighs and drumstick bones. Again, push the meat with skin downward as you cut. Chop through both drumstick bones 1" from the end joint. These bony pieces keep the end joints intact. Behold, you now have an inside out boneless whole bird! Trim fat and remove any hard or undesirable substances. Score the breast meat to tenderize it. Turn the bird right side out and shape it back into its best natural form. Reserve bones, fat, etc. for stock. The boneless fowl is now ready to be stuffed for a scrumptious gourmet feast. For advance preparation, refrigerate or freeze.

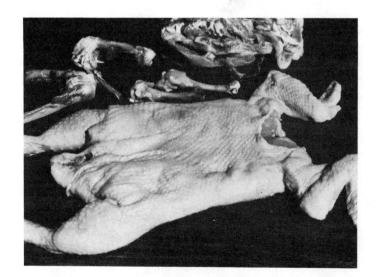

COOKING METHODS & UTENSILS

Stir-fry is best done in a wok, but it can be done in any large heavy-bottomed pot or skillet. The wok "releases" and imparts to food that desirable "wok hay" (meaning aroma, flavor or fragrance) which is unachievable when using other cookware. Heat a clean and dry utensil over high heat (or medium-high heat in some cases) until hot. Add oil. When oil is hot, but not smoking, add ginger and/or garlic (if used in recipe); stir a few times to extract flavor. Add well-drained vegetables or meat and stir briskly for the number of minutes specified in the recipe. Water should be added after the cooking has started and only when the vegetables have been well coated with oil and appear dry. Soft (or high water content) vegetables such as bok choy, mung bean sprouts and shredded jicama require the addition of little or no water. Always sprinkle one to two tablespoons of water at a time unless otherwise directed. The addition of water to the hot pan will erupt into steam and sizzle, imparting to food that special pan-fried flavor. Adding water at the beginning or in a large quantity would result in boiling and in an uninteresting and watery dish. Soft vegetables and meat should be stir-fried in their naturally exuded juices if possible. Hard (or low water content) vegetables such as lotus roots, potatoes and carrots require the addition of a small amount of water. Add 1/4 to 1/2 cup of water, depending on the quantity, to the vegetables after they have been thoroughly coated with oil and other seasonings or sauces. Cover pan and gently steam until tender. Semi-hard vegetables such as beans and peas can be stir-fried as soft vegetables or briefly steamed. Many of the cooking methods depend on the type of cutting. Shredded carrots, for instance, can be stir-fried as a soft vegetable, whereas chunk carrots must be treated as a hard vegetable. In stir-frying, all meat should be just delicately cooked and all vegetables should be tender-crisp. Never stir-fry a large quantity in a small pan all at once.

When cooking green vegetables, avoid repeatedly uncovering and covering with lid as this causes yellowing. If the vegetables are not to be served immediately and must be kept warm, do not cover pan completely. This, too, is to preserve the emerald green color. Overcooked or off-colored vegetables are most unappetizing.

GENERAL HINTS ON STIR-FRYING (CONTINUED)

Marinated thin chicken slices or minced chicken
(not beef or pork) can be very adhesive; it would
seem impossible to separate the pieces while stir-
frying. To eliminate this problem, simply add one
or two tablespoons of stock or water to the meat
and mix well just before cooking. For best results,
veal, pork, beef and seafood should be well drained
before marinating and warmed up to room temperature
before stir-frying.

Also, for a stronger and fresher aroma, add spices
(such as ground pepper, ground Szechwan peppercorns,
ground star anise and Chinese 5-spice) to meat and
mix well just before you are ready to cook.

GENERAL HINTS ON PAN-FRYING

Brown food in a small but generous amount of oil,
turning food to brown both sides until it is cooked
through. Temperatures may vary from medium-high to
medium-low. Always use a heavy-bottomed pan or wok.
Heat it until very hot, then reduce heat to maintain
a moderate temperature in most cases. Add oil; when
oil is hot, add food. This helps to prevent sticking and to give food its crispness. Turning over
can be a snap if the underside is properly browned.
This is essential when baking all types of pancakes.
Leave ample room between pieces of food for expansion and easy turning. If a sauce is to be added,
skim out the excess fat first. Specific directions
are given in the recipes.

Food is immersed in hot oil and cooked to an even brown, turning or rolling frequently. Temperatures vary. Deep fat frying requires special attention. The following is a list of common sense pointers. Nevertheless, they are worth remembering. Some pointers apply to pan-frying, stir-frying, steaming and boiling as well.

Although any heavy deep pan can be used, a deep-fryer with a wire basket is probably the best. The basket provides gentle lowering of food pieces at the same time for even cooking, and it is easily lifted up in case of bubbling over or excessive splattering. Fill the fryer with enough oil to cover food but not more than half full. Slowly heat oil, with basket in pan, until it reaches the desired temperature on the deep-fry thermometer. As soon as food is lowered into this hot fat, it is crusted to seal moisture in and oil out. If oil is not hot enough, food will sink to the bottom and sit, absorb excessive oil, and become scorched. Therefore, it is important that oil be at correct temperature before food is placed in it. If pastries look burned-brown on the outside and are raw on the inside, oil is too hot or heat may be too high. If pastries are grease-soaked, oil is not hot enough or heat may be too low. Perfectly fried food is crisp outside and non-greasy inside. Cooking times given in recipes are approximations. It is best to test a piece for doneness. Remove cooked food immediately to rack or absorbent paper to drain. Overcooking means greasier fried food or indigestible pastries. Skim out crumbs and bring oil back to required temperature before frying another batch. Always fry a few pieces at a time to allow free flow and motion. Pat watery food dry before immersing in oil.

Deep-frying is a full-time job. Never leave a pot of oil on a hot stove unattended. If oil is heated to the smoking point, it can catch fire. Never add water to burning oil in pan. If it is safe to do so, turn off heat and cover pan with the fryer lid--have the lid ready. Keep a quantity of baking soda handy to toss on kitchen fire at the base of the flames when applicable. Do not throw baking soda into a deep fat fire as this can cause splattering. It is good practice to have all necessary items at hand. Turn and remove food with a long-handled utensil. If chopsticks are employed, use only long wooden ones. Turn the handles of all pots and pans away from you and use the burners at the back of the stove if necessary. A splatter screen with a long handle can be a great aid. Above all, never permit children to cook with hot oil without supervision.

Deep-fried food, in some cases, is best deep-fried twice. Deep-fry in hot oil to cook the food the first time. Lift the food pieces out, reheat oil and refry the same pieces briefly for that extra crispness. This technique makes advance preparation possible--so you and your guests can enjoy hot and crispy food without too much last-minute cooking on your part.

Although oil can be strained, clarified and used again, the best deep-fried food comes from fresh clean oil. Fresh clean oil gives fried food that desirable crispness, taste and juiciness.

Filled pastries to be deep-fried should:

1. have a thicker crust, made with fresh flour. Stale flour, which has lost its natural oil and moisture, means crumbled dough and cracked pastries.
2. avoid oily and watery fillings.
3. be fried in fresh pure vegetable or peanut oil.
4. be at room temperature.
5. be fried as soon as they are made.
6. be covered with a splatter screen if crust cracks before fully cooked.
7. be added to oil only when oil has reached the required temperature. If oil is not hot enough, pastries will be grease-soaked. Then, as the temperature rises, some delicate pastries will crack, causing oil to splatter. Maintain an even cooking heat temperature (not the oil temperature; oil temperature will drop as soon as food is added.)

STEAMING: The common Chinese method is the metal tiered steamer or the bamboo steamer. The metal steamer has one or two steaming trays plus a large base pot which is partially filled with water when the whole unit is used for steaming. The base pot can be used to make soup, spaghetti or other foods in large quantities. The bamboo steamers are also known as bamboo trays or bamboo racks. They can be layered and placed in a wok filled with a small amount of water. Buns and dumplings or a plate of food are steamed on the steaming trays above boiling water.

Other devices can be easily assembled. Place the plate of food on wire rack in a large 12" or 14" skillet filled with water to below rack. Or, place a cylindical ring or an elevated rack (available at Oriental hardware stores) in a large pot having a domed lid (so steam can circulate freely over the food), then top this high-standing rack with a 10" cake rack. Fill the pot with a substantial amount of water. A plate of food or buns will then be placed on cake rack to steam. The water level should not be too high or too low. This is to prevent boiling over or drying out.

To steam: Cover with lid, bring water to a boil, place food on rack, start timing, and reduce heat to maintain a boil, sufficient to generate a strong and steady steam. Cooking time given in recipes may vary. The type of cookware and the stove being used all contribute to the length of the cooking time. Our experiments showed that food steamed in a deep bowl took considerably longer than food steamed in a shallow pyrex pie plate.

POACHING: Select a saucepan that fits the meat or whole fowl snugly. This is to reduce the amount of liquid needed to cover and cook the food, and results in about one quart of sauce to store or a richer and more flavorful broth. While poaching does not seem to dry out the meat as fast as roasting or deep-frying, it is best to keep the skin and fat on (if possible and appropriate). Excess fat and fatty skins can be removed after cooking. Bring the liquid or water to a boil, add food, then slow-simmer as directed in individual recipes. Because food is poached in bland clear liquid and with few ingredients added, the fresher the ingredients the better. The clear liquid should be reserved for soup or stock.

Slow-simmer techniques include braising, stewing and red-cooking.

Braised foods are first seared in fat and then simmered in a covered pan with a little liquid. After browning, skim out excess fat, add prepared sauce, cover with lid, and bring to a boil. Then reduce heat to maintain a somewhat strong simmer until the food is done, stirring occasionally and adding more liquid if needed. The wok or any large heavy-bottomed saucepan with a tight-fitting lid would be good cookware for braising. Braised foods are convenient do-ahead dishes. Let the cooked food stand to improve and ripen its flavor. A good example is the BRAISED SOY DUCK.

Stewed meats can be browned in fat or scalded briefly in boiling water, then simmered in liquid. Browning or scalding helps to seal in the natural juices. Stewing, on the average, requires a longer time than braising.

Red-cooking is a specialty in the Shanghai region of China. Red-cooked foods store well and can be eaten hot or cold. Red-cooking involves browning the meat by either pan-frying or deep-frying, then simmering in soy sauce, spices and sugar. Firm and/or dehydrated vegetables can also be added. Some cooks prefer to use dark soy sauce for the rich reddish color; some cooks prefer thin soy for its delicate flavor; and some cooks happily combine both. For convenience and economy, the sauces in these recipes are reduced to a minimum so there is no leftover sauce to store. The sauce in most recipes is cooked down to gravy consistency to glaze the food. Five-spice powder and star anise are favorite spices. Sugar, like the spices and soy sauce, adds mellowness and coloring. Red-cooked duck, red-cooked pork and red-cooked tongue are all rich extravagant gourmet dishes.

In China, roasting is done only commercially. It is not an integral part of home cooking; the oven does not exist in the home. A whole pig, pork strips called char shiu, chicken and duck are roasted to perfection by suspending the food in the center of the oven rather than laying it on the side. This is done so that food can absorb the even distribution of heat. It is therefore essential to have dry heat freely circulating around the food. With even the modern day household ovens, this is easier said than done. But an ingenious cook (and everyone can be an ingenious cook) or a handy man can surely invent a satisfactory device by suspending small "S" hooks or sturdy wire from the top rack of the oven to solve the problem. If this does not work, and it may not, then here are some second-choice suggestions which may work well.

a. Use rotisserie for unstuffed whole duck or chicken.

b. Use a vertical roaster to roast unstuffed whole duck or chicken, or hang char shiu strips around the roaster with small drapery hooks.

c. Elevate a roasting rack and lay food on top to roast. Turn food over to ensure even browning or crispness.

In any case, a shallow drip pan should be placed under the food with enough space between food and pan to allow heat circulation. Add just enough water to cover the bottom of the pan, adding more water as needed later on. The liquid will keep the drippings from burning and splattering, but too much liquid would result in steaming. If chicken is roasted horizontally, place the chicken with breast side down for most of the roasting time. The juice and oil from the back seep down to the breast, contributing to moist and juicy meat. Baste chicken from time to time if desired. When roasting duck on roasting rack, place duck with breast side up during most of the cooking period so the fatty layer under the skin can be cooked and melted away. There is no need to baste duck since the fat serves as a self-basting ingredient. If, at any time, any part gets too brown too fast, loosely lay a sheet of foil over the area. The foil should be removed during the last 5 to 10 minutes of cooking.

Chicken and pork strips roast beautifully in conventional household ovens without any complication. Our concern is duck roasting. Ideally, duck should be seared at about 425^0 F., then reduce the heat and roast at 350^0 F. to 375^0 F. until done. This method may work well commercially, but we found that fat content in duck combined with high heat (over 400° F.) can create excessive splattering and smoke.

One popular method is to roast at high temperature (about 400° F. for about 10 minutes) to sear the food, then reduce heat (around 350° F.) and roast until done. An alternative is to roast food at a steady temperature (around 350° F.) until done or finish at high temperature (around 400° F. for 10 minutes or so) for that crackling skin as in the case of duck. Our experiments showed that these two methods create little splattering and are therefore more practical for home roasting.

Every oven has its own temperament. You may have to perform a few tests to determine the best method and roasting time. Roasting time varies according to shape, weight, fat content, and whether or not the bird has been stuffed or sewn. Keep in mind also that the temperature indicator and the actual temperature inside the oven sometimes differ greatly. An oven thermometer may prove to be a sound investment. We can only conclude that experience is the best teacher.

BARBECUED RIBS, page 47

SO BAO, page 163

The Chinese-style soup can be a clear liquid stock with vegetables, seafoods and meat, or a slightly thickened soup with finely cut-up ingredients. Our soups are simple to prepare, economical, refreshing and satisfying. A bowl of hot soup can warm up a cold winter night and a bowl of refreshing soup makes a wonderful light meal for a hot summer day.

As stated in the stir-frying section, repeatedly uncovering and covering with lid can cause yellowing. This applies to vegetables in soup as well. Again, if the soup is not served immediately and must be kept hot, remove soup from heat and only partially cover pan to help retain the bright green color. Always bring the broth to a boil before adding vegetables, unless directed otherwise. Vegetables should be cooked as quickly as possible. Thinly sliced (less than 1/8" thick) raw meat should be added almost always last, and usually takes only 30 to 60 seconds to cook. If the meat is cooked perfectly, it will be tender and will (if marinated) have a mildly seasoned taste.

At times, marinated chicken meat or pork can be very adhesive. Always stir the meat well before adding it to the soup. This eliminates big stuck-together lumps which take much longer to cook and which can cause smaller pieces of meat and vegetables to overcook. This problem can be minimized by mixing one to two tablespoons of the soup stock into the meat just before adding it to the soup.

Should soy sauce be added to flavor the soup, use light soy sauce and use it discreetly. A bowl of brown soup does not whet the appetite.

Most clear-stock soups are light soups, such as REFRESHING VEGETABLE SOUP and LOTUS ROOT SOUP, and are normally served to accompany the family dinners. At an "old-fashioned" Chinese dinner, the soup is the beverage and is consumed from time to time throughout the meal. Hearty or thick soups, such as LONG LIFE NOODLE SOUP and FISH JOOK, are substantial enough for a one-pot light meal. See individual directions in recipes.

Purchase the wok of your choice. The most popular model preferred by my students is the 14-inch flat-bottomed carbon-steel wok with a long wooden handle. It is placed directly on the burner of the gas or electric stove (it is especially suitable for the electric stoves), without the supporting ring, thus providing higher heat which is essential when stir-frying many meat and vegetable dishes. It can also be used with the ring should one desire to do so.

Scour wok, inside and out, with sudsy detergent. Rinse well and wipe dry, then cure wok by following these simple steps:

1. Heat wok over high heat. Generally, a gas stove will do a better job. Tilt wok frequently so every part of the bowl will get darkened and the entire bowl is nearly smoking hot.

2. Generously grease the inside of bowl with oil or animal fat. Place wok on stove and heat until smoking hot, but not in flames. You need not cure the outside; the outside will take care of itself.

3. Completely wipe off oil with dry towel.

Repeat these three steps in the given order for a total of three or four times. Henceforth, do not wash wok with detergent; wash wok with hot water and a brush, and dry it over hot stove before storage. For added benefit, use wok to deep-fry the first two or three times. If wok gets rusty at any time, season it all over again.

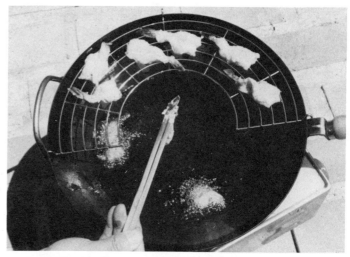

BUTTERFLY SHRIMP, page 92

All Chinese or Oriental ingredients are available at Chinese markets, other Oriental shops and increasingly at the supermarkets. Good food comes from its quality components. It is essential to use choice and fresh ingredients. Substitute any disagreeable ingredient with a similar product or omit it from recipe if possible and necessary. It is the cook's responsibility to select agreeable and edible ingredients.

Almond powder. A pure white powder available in 10-oz. jars. Keep almond powder at room temperature.

Baby young corn. Sweet and succulent tiny corn ears 2 to 4 inches long, canned in salt and water. Available at Oriental shops, delicatessens and some supermarkets.

Bamboo leaves. These leaves are dried and neatly stacked and tied. They must be thoroughly soaked, washed and scalded.

Bamboo shoots. Canned bamboo shoots in various sizes are available. Immerse unused shoots in water; keep in refrigerator. Change water daily to preserve freshness.

Bean curd cake. See tofu.

Black bean sauce with chili. It is a hot and spicy sauce made from black beans, chili, salt and oil, a good substitute for salted black beans and hot chili combination.

Bok choy. Bok choy is a white-stalked and green-leafed vegetable similar to the green Swiss chard. There are two main varieties sold in the United States (more than 2 varieties in China)--the large broad-stalked type and the small variety, bok choy sum, with a tender central stem (the heart) and very few green leaves. The latter is more desirable and is sold only in Chinatown. Bok choy will keep for a few days in the refrigerator.

Char shiu. These glazed roasted pork strips can be purchased from Oriental delicatessens and some markets. See CANTONESE ROASTED PORK, page 48.

Chee hou sauce. Made from sugar, vinegar, soy beans, water, salt, flour, malted rice, chili and spices. It keeps almost indefinitely refrigerated.

Chicken broth. The chicken broth used throughout this book will be the undiluted commercially prepared high quality chicken broth or home-cooked broth having at least the same strength.

Other substitutes may require an adjustment in quantity and/or flavor.

Chili oil. Its ingredients are salad oil and hot pepper. Use sparingly. For homemade chili oil, see recipe.

Chili peppers. See dried red hot chili peppers.

Chili powder. Some brands are hot and some are mild. Use sparingly or season to taste.

Chinese barbecue sauce. This sauce is usually made from beans, flour, soy sauce, sugar, salt and coloring. It is available in one-pound jars. Keeps well in closed jar in refrigerator. At present, there are different brands on the market; some are better than others, and some contain fish. Read label before purchase.

Chinese chives. These chives have flat green stalks that look more like garlic stalks than scallion stalks. They have a mild garlic flavor, adding a distinctive spicy taste to food. Chinese chives are often used with eggs, noodles and meat.

Chinese five-spice. This consists of ground peppercorns, anise, fennel seeds, cinnamon and cloves. It is available in small plastic bags in all Oriental shops and in spice-sized jars in some supermarkets. For a stronger and fresher aroma, add spices (such as ground pepper, ground star anise, ground Szechwan peppercorns and 5-spice) to meat and mix well just before cooking.

Chinese pork sausage. There are liver sausages, beef sausages and pork sausages. For fillings and toppings, pork sausages are often used. Rinse sausages and pat dry before using.

Chinese white radish (Chinese turnip). These turnips are 6 to 8 inches long, 3 inches across with mild, crisp, white flesh. Daikon would be a good substitute.

Chinese yard-long beans. Tender stringless green beans measure 18 to 24 inches long. Available in the summer.

Cloud ears (black fungus). A dried small ruffled grayish brown fungus. Sold in small packages in various sizes. They must be soaked, thoroughly rinsed, squeezed dry, and tough stems must be removed. The texture is slightly crunchy.

Coriander. It is also called Chinese parsley or cilantro, used for seasoning and garnish. Buy fresh or freeze-dried (in spice-sized jars).

Dried Chinese mushrooms. Different quality dried mushrooms are available in cellophane bags of various sizes. Mushrooms should be sun dried for one day before lengthy storage. To use in recipes, soak, remove stems and wash thoroughly.

Dried Chinese red dates (jujube). A small fruit
used for flavoring. Adds a touch of sweetness
to food. Soak to soften before cooking.

Dried Chinese tangerine peel. Well-aged peels
impart the best flavor. Soak to soften before
using.

Dried red hot chili peppers. The dried chili peppers
used in this book are small dried chili peppers,
1-1/2 to 2 inches in length, such as japones
(a Japanese chili). If other large dried peppers
are used, adjust the amount to your own taste.
Store dried peppers in a clean dry jar
at room temperature. Chili peppers,
fresh or dried, can irritate tender
and sensitive skin and cause a burning
sensation. Wash your hands thoroughly
immediately after handling these peppers.
The fumes from browning dried hot chili in oil
can also be very irritating and can cause one
to cough temporarily. This condition can be
minimized by cooking in a well ventilated space,
with fan on and windows open. Brown peppers
over low heat and add other ingredients to wok
as soon as peppers are darkened. If desired,
dried hot peppers and sauce (such as salted
black beans, ground bean sauce, hoisin sauce,
sweet bean sauce, etc.) in recipe can be re-
placed by chili paste with garlic, black bean

sauce with chili, or Szechwan hot bean sauce.

Dried salted duck gizzards. Fresh cleaned duck
gizzards preserved with salt, soy sauce and wine.
Mostly used to flavor soups. Sliced cooked dried
gizzards can be eaten as finger-food for snacks.

Dried shrimp. Cooked, salted, shelled and dried
shrimp is a favorite ingredient added to fillings
and toppings. Soak to soften, pick over and
rinse well before using.

Fish sauce (or fish soy). An extract from fresh fish,
contains salt, derived proteins and water. It is
a thin sauce. Available in different sized bottles.

Ginger. One slice of ginger means one piece of ginger
about the size of a quarter.

Glutinous rice. This is often labeled as sweet rice.
It is a short-grain rice, sticky, used for fried
rice, pastries and stuffings.

Glutinous rice flour. Flour milled from glutinous
rice. It is available in one-pound packages
and is sometimes labeled as sweet rice flour.
(Note that "glutinous rice flour--*fried*" does
not have the same consistency and texture as
glutinous rice flour and should not be substituted.) Sift all imported flours.

Golden needles (lily buds). Dried lily buds are
about 3" long with a pale gold color. Soak
only until softened, pinch off hard stems and
squeeze dry. Lily buds add a different unique

flavor to steamed chicken, vegetarian foods and other dishes.

Ground bean sauce. This sauce is made from yellow beans, flour, salt and water. Available in 16-oz. cans. It keeps well in closed jar in refrigerator.

Hoisin sauce. Its ingredients are yellow beans, salt, flour, sugar, vinegar and food color. Available in cans or jars. It keeps well in closed glass jar under refrigeration.

Hot Chinese barbecue sauce. The ingredients are sugar, soy sauce, hoisin sauce, catsup, black beans, hot pepper oil, wine, garlic, ginger and spices. Available in 8-oz. jars.

Jicama. This root vegetable is crisp and crunchy. It makes an excellent substitute for water chestnuts or bamboo shoots. Unpeeled, it keeps well in refrigerator. Cut as much as needed.

Lemon sauce. Made from sugar, lemon, vinegar and salt. Store in refrigerator after opening. Some brand names are slightly bitter and some are pleasantly tart and sweet.

Lily buds. See golden needles.

Lotus root. Fresh lotus roots are available at Oriental markets. The appearance is similar to a sectioned long balloon tied by 2 or 3 knots. A cross section displays round holes with different diameters. Canned lotus root can be used in soup, but not in a stir-fried dish.

Lumpia wrappers (also called Chinese spring roll skins). These wrappers are paper-thin and non-stick, so they can be separated without tearing. Deep-fried, they are extra crisp and light. They are made with flour, water, eggs, sugar and salt. The size is usually 8" square. These are all-purpose wrappers, good for egg rolls, lumpia, and chagio.

Oil. Peanut oil is the first choice. Other quality vegetable oils may be used.

Oyster sauce. Its ingredients are oyster extracts, water, salt, starch, acetic acid, sodium benzoate and caramel. Store in refrigerator after opening.

Pork. Over-the-counter ground pork contains too much fat. It is better to buy a piece of boneless pork butt, trim off some fat, cut into small strips, partially freeze until firm, but not solid, then grind. To chop with the Chinese cleaver or food processor, omit freezing. It takes only seconds to mince in the food processor.

Preserved dried pork. This "Chinese bacon" is also known as Chinese-style cured pork belly strips. It is sold by the pound. Rinse well before using.

Preserved salted turnip. Salted turnips are sold by weight in plastic bags. Most likely they are already sliced into strips and sometimes the strips are rolled up into a knot. To store, keep in dry clean jar at room temperature. They will last for a long, long time. Unroll, soak and rinse clean before using.

Preserved Szechwan mustard. It is also known as Szechwan kohlrabi, canned in spices, hot and spicy. Store in clean glass jar; will keep at room temperature for about 12 months.

Red bean paste. A ready-to-use paste, made from red beans, sugar and water. Available in 18-oz. cans.

Salted black beans. Black beans preserved with salt and sometimes with bits of ginger and tangerine peel added. Store in jar at room temperature. Available in plastic bags. Rinse off salt before using.

Salted duck eggs. Fresh duck eggs preserved with a coat of salty ashes. The yolk is solid and red. If hard-boiled, the yolk displays a few drops of oil. Salted eggs can be preserved as follows: Dissolve coarse kosher salt, about 1 tablespoon per egg, in boiling water; cool completely. Then place eggs in a glass jar and pour salt water over eggs to cover. Keep jar in a cool place. Eggs will be ready in about 40 days.

Sesame oil. This is Oriental sesame oil, made from toasted sesame seeds. Widely available at the supermarkets. It adds aroma to food.

Sesame seeds. There are white and black sesame seeds. Available in plastic bags. To toast white sesame seeds: Put seeds in a clean, dry, heavy-bottomed saucepan and toast on stove over low heat, stirring often until golden. Or toast in a slow oven, stirring often until golden.

Sherry. Any kind of sherry or Chinese wine may be used. Cream sherry adds a touch of sweetness to shrimp and beef, thereby eliminating the addition of sugar.

Soy sauces. Soy sauces are classified as thin (or light) soy and dark (or black) soy. Thin soy is made from yellow beans, flour, salt and water; dark soy has molasses added. Thin soy is preferred for table condiment and soups; dark soy adds a deeper color to food.

Star anise and ground star anise. Its Chinese name means "eight corners". It has a very strong flavor. Break off individual pods. Two to four pods are usually sufficient. To powder anise: Grind star anise in blender until powdery, then sift. Discard coarse residue. Store powder in jar for use. See Chinese 5-spice also.

Straw mushrooms. Peeled straw mushrooms canned in salt and water. Available in 15-oz. cans.

Subgum sauce. Made from yellow beans, flour, sugar, vinegar, salt and food color. Available in 1-lb. cans. Sometimes it is misleadingly labeled as "bean sauce".

Sweet bean sauce. Made from soy beans, flour, sugar, spices and bean sauce. It is not very sweet, but actually somewhat salty.

Sweet rice. See glutinous rice.

Szechwan hot bean sauce. A spicy thick sauce made from beans, red chili and spices.

Taro. A starchy tuber found in the vegetable section of Oriental markets. See TARO CAKE recipe.

Tofu (fresh bean curd). It is also called "soy bean curd cake" or "soy bean cake". Its texture can be firm, medium-firm, soft, or very soft.

Vermicelli. Vermicelli are also called bean threads or cellophane noodles. Made from mung bean starch. It is an ingredient added to many vegetarian or meat dishes. Deep-fried vermicelli are tossed in fresh salads.

Water chestnuts. Fresh or canned water chestnuts can be used in all recipes. However, fresh water chestnuts are much better. Fresh water chestnuts are crunchy and sweet, similar to fresh apples in September. Peel off the covering, rinse well, then eat them raw for snacks.

Wet bean curd (nam yu). This is fermented red bean curd. Small blocks of pressed reddish bean curd and some sauce are canned in various sized containers. The added ingredients are salt, spices and wine. Upon opening, store in jar under refrigeration. Another type of fermented bean curd is *fu yu*, which is beige colored and has a very different flavor and taste.

Wheat starch. Available in 1-lb. packages. Sift upon opening a new package.

White rice flour. This is flour milled from long-grain rice. Natural food stores carry a large supply of rice flour and it is labeled as "white rice flour". Imported rice flour is often labeled as "rice flour". It is not to be confused with the "sweet rice flour" which is a glutinous flour. Sift imported rice flour with the finest meshed sifter. Imported rice flour and the domestic product differ in dryness and texture. It may be necessary to adjust the amount of liquid to be used. If possible, use imported rice flour. Domestic rice flour is usually much too grainy.

Winter melon. Most winter melons are huge, weighing more than 30 pounds. The exterior is light green, covered with white powder. Buy it by the slice (except when doing a melon pond); keep in refrigerator. Whole melons will keep for months through the winter. Small mature melons are used to make the famous whole winter melon pond.

Won ton skins. Round skins are available in Oriental

markets and noodle factories. Square skins are available at most supermarkets as well as Oriental markets. Freeze or refrigerate well-wrapped skins. If round won ton skins are not available, cut the square skins with scissors or a doughnut cutter. Doughnut cutter size is perfect for hors d'oeuvres. Deep-fry the left-over corners, crumble, and add to fresh salad. Or, sprinkle cinnamon-sugar over deep-fried won ton skins and serve for snacks. For homemade won ton skins, spring roll skins, noodles or pot sticker skins: Mix together two cups all-purpose flour, two large eggs (beaten), 1/4 teaspoon salt and about three tablespoons water; knead into a smooth non-sticky dough. Cover with a dampened towel and let it rest for 20 minutes. Roll out the dough, on lightly floured surface, to desired thinness (even paper-thin thickness for that deep-fried crispness); cut into desired size and shape. Spread on counter to dry briefly until firm. Do not overdry; the dough will curl and crack. Lightly sprinkle cornstarch over noodles or skins, then wrap for storage.

SILVER-THREAD SAUSAGE ROLLS, page 166

FIN-SHAPED SHIU MAI, page 155

Many Chinese ingredients are so vaguely named as to mean almost anything to anyone. Make photo copies of these pages. Carry them with you when you shop so you get the exact items that you need.

almond powder	杏仁霜		Chinese five-spice	五香粉
baby young corn	玉米筍		Chinese pork sausage	白油腸
bamboo leaves	竹葉		Chinese white radish	白蘿蔔
bamboo shoots	竹筍		Chinese yard-long beans	豆角
bean curd or tofu	豆腐		cloud ears or black fungus	雲耳
black bean sauce with chili	香豉辣醬		dried Chinese mushrooms	冬菇
bok choy	白菜心		dried Chinese red dates	紅棗
char shiu	叉燒		dried Chinese tangerine peel	陳皮
chee hou sauce	柱侯醬		dried red hot chili pepper	乾辣椒
chili oil	辣油		dried salted duck gizzards	乾鴨胃
Chinese barbecue sauce	燒烤醬		dried shrimp	蝦米
Chinese chives	韮菜		fish sauce or fish soy	魚露

glutinous rice or sweet rice	糯米	salted black beans	豆豉
glutinous rice flour or sweet rice flour	糯米粉	salted duck eggs	鹹蛋
golden needles or lily buds	金針	sesame oil	芝蔴油
ground bean sauce	磨原豉	light soy sauce 鮮抽 dark soy sauce 老頭抽	
hoisin sauce	海鮮醬	star anise	八角
hot Chinese barbecue sauce	辣燒烤醬	subgum sauce	什錦醬
jicama	薯葛	sweet bean sauce	甜麵醬
lemon sauce	檸檬醬	Szechwan hot bean sauce	辣豆瓣醬
lotus root	蓮藕	taro	芋
lumpia wrappers	春捲皮	vermicelli or bean threads	粉絲
oyster sauce	蠔油	wet bean curd	南乳
preserved dried pork	臘肉	wheat starch	澄麵粉
preserved salted turnip	冲菜	white rice flour	粘米粉
preserved Szechwan mustard	四川搾菜	winter melon	冬瓜
red bean paste	紅豆沙	won ton skins	雲吞皮

MEATS

PORK SPARERIBS SIMMERED IN BARBECUE SAUCE
4 or 5 servings

3 lb. pork spareribs, chopped in 1-1/2" chunks, parboiled until just cooked through, rinsed and drained

1 to 2 tablespoons oil

2 slices peeled ginger

1 green onion, minced

Sauce: mix

> 1/4 teaspoon Chinese 5-spice
>
> 1/4 teaspoon salt
>
> 1 teaspoon cornstarch
>
> 2 tablespoons Chinese barbecue sauce or chee hou sauce
>
> 1 tablespoon *each* dark soy sauce and Chinese rice wine
>
> 1 teaspoon ground bean sauce
>
> 1/2 cup *each* chicken broth (or other stock) and water (add more water if needed during cooking)
>
> 1 teaspoon sesame oil

Heat wok or a heavy-bottomed large pot until hot. Add oil. When oil is hot, add ginger and stir until brown. Add meat; stir and toss until coated with oil and golden brown. Add sauce; cover and simmer over medium-low heat for about 40 minutes, stirring occasionally. (The sauce should have a gravy consistency; otherwise, uncover and cook over higher heat until it's gravy-like.) Skim out as much oil as you can. Add onion; toss and serve. This is a delicious way to cook spareribs when the oven is not available.

STEAMED PORK HASH WITH SALTED EGGS
3 or 4 servings

1   lb. ground pork (buy boneless pork, then mince)
3   salted duck eggs, separated, cut yolks into quarters
1/8 teaspoon ground pepper
1/8 teaspoon salt, more or less, depending on the saltiness of the eggs
1   teaspoon sesame oil
1   tablespoon dark soy sauce
1   green onion, chopped

Mix pork, egg whites, pepper, salt, sesame oil and soy sauce. Spread over a 9" pyrex pie plate. Garnish with egg yolks and onion (or add onion the last minute of cooking to get a nice green color). Steam over boiling water until cooked, about 25 minutes. Serve with rice.

Note. If eggs are preserved with a coat of ashes, scrape this preserving material off, rinse clean, then shell.

BASIC STIR-FRIED PORK
(all purpose)

1   lb. pork (trimmed weight), sliced across grain, or cut into shreds, marinated in:
    1/2 tablespoon Chinese barbecue sauce (hoisin sauce, ground bean sauce, sweet bean sauce, or chee hou sauce)*
    1/2 teaspoon salt
    1   tablespoon cornstarch
    1/2 teaspoon *each* sesame oil and sherry
    1   teaspoon soy sauce (use thin soy if you like a light color)
2   to 3 tablespoons oil
1   green onion, cut into long thin shreds
1   slice ginger, crushed (or 1 large clove garlic, crushed)

Heat wok until hot. Add oil; stir a few times. Add ginger or garlic and brown to extract flavor. Add pork and stir-fry until done, 3 to 5 minutes. Add onion shreds; toss. Serve as a meat dish or add meat to stir-fried vegetables and mix well.

Variation: Substitute turkey breast tenderloins for pork and add 2 tablespoons chicken broth to marinade. Stir-fry over medium-high heat as directed.

* Each sauce will give a different flavor.

TWICE-COOKED PORK
2 servings

2   lb. boneless Boston butt or pork shoulder; leave it whole, do not trim fat

2   slices peeled ginger

1   star anise

1   teaspoon salt

1   green bell pepper, cut in 1" pieces

1/2   green onion, cut in 1" lengths

1   clove garlic, minced

2   or 3 dried red chili peppers*, seeded and halved or coarsely crushed for spicier taste

Sauce: mix

    1-1/2   tablespoons sweet bean sauce

    1   tablespoon dark soy sauce

    1/2   tablespoon sherry

    1   teaspoon *each* sugar and sesame oil

    3   tablespoons reserved liquid (see below) or clear chicken broth

Parboil pork for 5 minutes. Drain, rinse, and drain again. Place pork, ginger, anise, salt and enough fresh boiling water to cover most of the pork in a saucepan. Cover with lid and cook over medium-low heat until tender, about 1-1/2 hours. Cool meat, then place in refrigerator to chill until firm for easy slicing. Skim out fat from liquid and save the liquid for soup, stew or sauces. When ready to stir-fry, trim fat from pork, and cut *half* of the meat into bite-sized thin slices. Save the other half for another meal.

Stir-fry green pepper in 1 to 1-1/2 tablespoons hot oil and a pinch of salt until pepper is crisp-tender, 1-1/2 to 2 minutes, sprinkling 1 to 2 tablespoons of water around the sides of wok if needed. Set pepper aside.

Add another 1 to 1-1/2 tablespoons oil to wok. When hot, add chili peppers and stir until brown, about 20 seconds. Add garlic; stir once or twice, then add pork and toss until heated through. Add sauce, green pepper and green onion. Stir until bubbly. Add more sugar or salt if needed.

* You may substitute 1 tablespoon hot bean sauce or hot bean paste for the chili peppers. Add bean sauce to flavor the oil or mix the bean sauce into the sauce mixture, and replace the dark soy sauce by 1 tablespoon reserved liquid. See dried red hot chili pepper in INGREDIENTS.

SZECHWAN-STYLE STIR-FRIED PORK
4 servings

oil for cooking

1/2 to 3/4 cup sliced bamboo shoots or sliced celery

1 2" cube preserved Szechwan mustard (kohlrabi), shredded (you should get 1/4 to 1/3 cup)

1 carrot, peeled, sliced, parboiled for 3 minutes (or 1 small red bell pepper, cut in thin strips)

3/4 lb. (net weight) all lean boneless pork butt or shoulder, shredded, marinated in:

a sprinkle of ground pepper

1/8 teaspoon salt

1 tablespoon cornstarch

2 teaspoons thin soy sauce

Sauce: mix

1 teaspoon cornstarch

1/2 teaspoon sugar

1 tablespoon cream sherry

1/2 cup chicken stock or water

Set wok over high heat until very hot. Add 1-1/2 to 2 tablespoons oil; swirl around a few times. Add pork and kohlrabi; stir-fry until cooked through, 3 to 3-1/2 minutes. Remove and set aside. Reheat wok, then add bamboo shoots and carrot. Stir and toss for 1 to 1-1/2 minutes or until vegetables are crisp-tender. Sprinkle 1 to 2 tablespoons water over vegetables as you stir-fry. Add sauce and stir until thickened. Mix in meat with kohlrabi. Serve with rice.

Szechwan preserved kohlrabi is mildly spicy and salty. It is best to serve a mildly seasoned meatless stir-fried vegetable dish as accompaniment.

STIR-FRIED PORK IN BEAN SAUCE
3 or 4 servings

oil for cooking

1   large or 2 small cloves garlic, minced

1   green onion, finely cut into bits

10   oz. (net weight), all lean pork butt, cut into shreds, marinated in:

    1   tablespoon cornstarch

    1/4   scant teaspoon salt

    1   teaspoon *each* thin soy sauce, sesame oil and sherry

Sauce: mix

    1/2   teaspoon cornstarch

    1   teaspoon sugar

    1   tablespoon cream sherry

   1-1/2   tablespoons ground bean sauce

    1/3   cup chicken broth

Heat wok until very hot. Add 1-1/2 to 2 tablespoons oil; swirl to coat wok. Add garlic; stir a few times. Add pork and stir-fry over high heat until just cooked through, about 2-1/2 minutes. Pour in sauce. Continue to toss and stir until bubbly and thickened. Add green onion. Mix and serve. Total cooking time takes 3 to 3-1/2 minutes. For variation, substitute turkey thigh meat for pork. Stir-fry over medium-high heat.

ANISE WHITE HAM
good for cold cuts

3   lb. leg of pork

2   tablespoons salt

Sauce:

    1/2   onion, cut in large wedges

    2   cloves garlic

    2   star anise

    1   teaspoon salt

   water, enough to cover meat

Rinse meat clean and pat dry. Do not cut off fat. Rub 2 tablespoons salt all over pork. Leave in refrigerator for 2 to 3 days. Rinse salt off pork. Drop meat into a large pot of boiling water and bring to a boil. Drain and rinse meat with cold water. Place meat in a heavy saucepan (one that holds the meat snugly). Add sauce and bring to a boil. Then reduce heat to medium-low and simmer until tender, 1-1/2 to 2 hours. The meat should be tender but should still hold its shape. Pour sauce through a strainer; discard residue. Save sauce for gravy, for cooking other meat or vegetables, or add it to the stockpot. Trim fat and serve meat for dinner. Or, chill meat in refrigerator until cold and firm, then slice and use for cold-cuts. Meat can also be added to fried rice or used in fillings.

BARBECUED RIBS
4-6 servings

3   to 3-1/4 lb. pork spareribs or pork loin country-style ribs

2   tablespoons Chinese barbecue sauce

1   tablespoon *each* dark soy sauce and sherry

1/4   teaspoon Chinese 5-spice

1/2   teaspoon salt

1   teaspoon sesame oil

2   teaspoons cornstarch

Marinate ribs in mixture of barbecue sauce, soy sauce, sherry, 5-spice, salt, sesame oil and cornstarch for at least 3 hours or overnight.

Arrange ribs in a single layer on an oven rack. Place a large roasting pan, filled with 1/4" water, 4 to 6 inches below rack. Roast at 375° F. for 35 minutes. Turn ribs over and roast until done, about 30 minutes more.

Chop ribs into 1-1/2" chunks. Serve with plum sauce or sweet and sour sauce.

See photo on page 28.

SPARERIBS WITH BLACK BEANS
3 or 4 servings

1-1/2   lb. fresh (not frozen; frozen meat is too watery for steaming) pork loin country-style spareribs

1/2   teaspoon salt

pinch ground pepper

2   tablespoons cornstarch

1   tablespoon salted black beans, rinsed, drained, mashed

2   cloves garlic, minced

2   tablespoons dark soy sauce

1   tablespoon sherry

2   or 3 slices peeled ginger, shredded

fresh coriander or 1 green onion cut in 1-1/2" lengths

Chop ribs into 1-1/2" chunks. Trim off fat and discard large bones that are too difficult to chop. Combine meat, salt, ground pepper, cornstarch, black beans, garlic, soy sauce and sherry; mix well. Let marinate for an hour.

Place meat in a large (10" or larger) heatproof plate. Garnish with ginger and coriander. Steam over boiling water until meat is cooked through and the gravy is thickened, 20 to 25 minutes. This is an excellent meat dish to serve with rice.

CANTONESE ROASTED PORK
all-purpose roasted meat

3 lb. (net weight) boneless pork butt or shoulder
1 tablespoon honey or syrup for brushing
Marinade: mix

    1/8 teaspoon ground pepper
  1-1/4 teaspoons salt
     2 tablespoons sugar
     2 tablespoons wet bean curd, well-mashed
     1 tablespoon each Chinese barbecue sauce
       and sherry
     1 clove garlic, finely minced
     1 teaspoon sesame oil

Trim off some fat from pork, but do not trim off all the fat as it keeps the lean meat moist and tender. Excess fat can be trimmed after cooking. Cut meat along the grain into strips about 8" long with a cross section approximately 2"x2". Marinate pork overnight in refrigerator. Suspend meat strips from top rack or arrange meat strips in a single layer on rack. Place a large roasting pan, filled with 1/4" water, 4 to 6 inches below rack. Roast at 375° F. for 45 to 60 minutes or until all sides are lightly brown and the meat is cooked through. If roasting on rack, turn strips over after the first 25-30 minutes. Do not overcook. Adjust temperature or roasting time to yield the best result. Brush hot meat with honey. Slice before serving.

Char shiu, as it is called in Cantonese, is a gourmet delicacy. It is also used to make fillings or added to stir-fried vegetables, fried rice, or chow mein. Char shiu can be stored in the refrigerator for 5 days or frozen for a longer period. Keep some in your freezer for "emergencies".

RED-HEARTED MEAT BALLS
15 meat balls

3/4 lb. lean pork butt or pork shoulder

1/4 cup dried shrimp, soaked to soften, picked over

1 tablespoon cornstarch

2 tablespoons minced green onion

2 teaspoons fish sauce (or thin soy sauce)

1 salted duck egg, see below

fresh coriander sprigs

Scrape preserving materials off egg. Wash and shell. Cut yolk into 15 pieces. Reserve egg white.

Grind or preferably chop together the pork and shrimp. Add cornstarch, green onion, fish sauce and egg white; mix well. Roll mixture into 15 meat balls, enclosing a piece of yolk in each center. Arrange meat balls on lightly greased heatproof plate. Garnish with coriander. Steam over boiling water until cooked through, 18 to 20 minutes. Serve hot for dim sum or as a meat dish for dinner.

BEAN CURD CHOW YUK
3 servings

oil for cooking

1 clove garlic, crushed

1 green onion, cut in fine shreds 1-1/2" long

3/4 lb. (net weight) all lean pork butt, shredded, marinated in:

1 tablespoon cornstarch

1/4 teaspoon salt

a sprinkle of ground pepper

2 teaspoons thin soy sauce

1 teaspoon *each* sesame oil and sherry

Sauce: mix

1/2 teaspoon sugar

1 teaspoon *each* cornstarch and sherry

2 teaspoons wet bean curd

1/3 cup water

Set wok over high heat until hot. Add 1-1/2 to 2 tablespoons oil and garlic. Stir and brown to extract garlic essence. Add pork; stir-fry until just cooked through, about 3 minutes. Add sauce and onion and continue to stir and toss until thickened. Serve with rice.

HAM AND BEANS
4 or 5 servings

1 lb. pinto beans, soaked overnight, rinsed
1 to 2 lb. ham hock or ham with bone, skin and
   fat removed
water for cooking
1 teaspoon sesame oil
salt and ground pepper to taste
Thickener: mix
      2 tablespoons all-purpose flour
      2 tablespoons water

Place beans and ham in a fairly large heavy saucepan. Add enough water to cover the beans and
bring to a full boil. Reduce heat to medium-low
and cook, covered, until the beans are tender,
about an hour. Stir beans occasionally and add
more water if needed. Remove ham from beans.
Discard bones and cut meat into bite-sized pieces.
Return meat to beans. Slowly add thickener to
beans while stirring until the desired consistency
is obtained. It may be necessary for you to add
more thickener or water. Add sesame oil, salt and
pepper.

STEAMED PORK WITH RED BEAN CURD
4 to 6 servings

2 lb. pork butt or country-style spareribs, cut
   in 1-1/2" cubes
3 slices peeled ginger, slivered
2 tablespoons cornstarch
1/4 teaspoon salt
1/8 teaspoon ground pepper
1 green onion, cut in 1" lengths for garnish
1 tablespoon thin soy sauce
1 tablespoon wet bean curd
1 tablespoon wet bean curd liquid (from the same
   can; see wet bean curd in INGREDIENTS)
1/2 tablespoon sherry (cream sherry would be good
   and is sweet)

Drop pork into boiling water and boil for a few
minutes. Rinse, drain, discard fat and large bones.

Mix all ingredients; place in a 9" or 10" pyrex pie
plate. Cover and steam until almost done. Garnish
with onion and continue steaming until cooked, about
45 minutes in all. Serve with hot cooked rice.

To serve for dim sum, serve in small dishes with
about 6 pieces per plate.

RED-COOKED PORK
5 or 6 servings

3 lb. pork butt roast or country-style spare-ribs, cut in 1-1/2" chunks

2 tablespoons brown sugar

2 tablespoons dark soy sauce

1-1/2 inches stick cinnamon

2 or 3 slices peeled ginger root

3 tablespoons sherry or Chinese rice wine

1 star anise

2 green onions, white parts only

3 tablespoons wet bean curd

1 cup water, more if needed

garnish, see FANCY GARNISHES

Add pork to a large pot of boiling water and bring to a boil over high heat (about 6 minutes), stirring twice or so. Pour off hot water and rinse with cold water. Drain.

Put all the ingredients in a heavy-bottomed pot. Bring to a boil. Reduce heat to medium-low and simmer until tender for about 55 minutes, stirring occasionally. The meat should be tender and "red", and the sauce should be thick (like gravy). Skim out fat. Spoon into server. Garnish and serve with hot cooked rice. If the sauce is too watery, cook over high heat, uncovered, until a gravy consistency remains.

Leftover meat can be used to make fried rice, fillings, or sandwiches. Or, cut pork into slices and serve as appetizer.

Do not use pork loin roast or cut out all the fat; the meat will be "dry". You can trim off the excess fat after the meat is cooked.

SWEET AND SOUR PORK--GOURMET RECIPE
4 servings

oil for deep-frying

1 lb. (net weight) boneless lean pork butt or
country-style pork loin, cut in 1-1/2" cubes,
marinated for at least 2 hours in:

    1/2 teaspoon salt

    2 teaspoons *each* cornstarch, thin soy
sauce and sherry

    1/8 teaspoon ground pepper

Sweet and Sour Sauce:

    2 to 3 tablespoons oil

    1 slice peeled ginger, crushed

    1/2 *each* green and red bell pepper, diced
(or substitute parboiled carrot slices
for red pepper and onion slices for
green pepper)

    1 20-oz. can pineapple chunks (or lychees)
in heavy syrup, drained, reserve syrup

    1/2 teaspoon sesame oil

mix together:

    1 tablespoon *each* brown sugar and
cornstarch

    1/8 teaspoon salt or to taste

    1/2 cup reserved syrup

    2 heaping tablespoons catsup

    2-1/2 tablespoons white vinegar

Coating: mix to make a somewhat thick paste

    4 tablespoons cornstarch

    2 tablespoons all-purpose flour

pinch of salt

about 3-1/2 tablespoons water

Add paste to marinated pork; mix well. Deep-fry
meat in 360° F. oil until golden and cooked through,
about 3 minutes. Remove with skimmer. Reheat oil
and refry the meat for another 30 to 60 seconds to
give the meat that extra crispness. Remove meat to
drain oil.

Heat wok until hot. Add 2 tablespoons oil and a
pinch of salt. When hot, add green and red peppers
and stir-fry for 1 to 1-1/2 minutes. Sprinkle one
to two teaspoons of water over peppers, if needed.
Remove with slotted spoon, leaving oil in wok. Set
peppers aside.

Reheat wok with oil. Add ginger; stir to brown.
Pour in sauce; cook and stir until thickened. Add
pineapple and heat it through. Remove wok from
heat. Add peppers, meat, sesame oil and another
2 to 3 teaspoons oil (optional and only if you

SWEET AND SOUR PORK--GOURMET RECIPE
(continued)

wish the dish to have a shiny appearance). Quickly toss several times. Serve at once.

Variation: Substitute pork spareribs for the
pork butt. Chop, through the bone, into bite-
sized pieces. Marinate and cook as directed
above. Serve deep-fried spareribs as appetizers
without the sauce, or serve as sweet and sour
spareribs with the sauce.

ONION BEEF
4 servings

2   slices peeled ginger, slivered

1   bunch green onions, cut in 1-1/2" long shreds

1/4   to 1/2 teaspoon sugar, according to taste

1   teaspoon sesame oil

2   to 3 teaspoons toasted white sesame seeds, see
    sesame seeds in INGREDIENTS

1   lb. flank steak, thinly sliced (less than 1/8")
    across the grain, marinated in:

    1/2   teaspoon beef bouillon powder
    (optional)

    1-1/2   tablespoons cornstarch

    1/2   teaspoon salt

    2   teaspoons cooking oil

    1/2   tablespoon *each* thin soy sauce and
    cream sherry

Heat wok, then add 2 to 3 tablespoons oil. When hot,
add ginger; brown to extract flavor. Add beef and
stir-fry until almost done. Add sugar, sesame oil
and green onions; mix well. Spoon into server,
sprinkle with sesame seeds, and serve.

Variation: Thinly slice 1 yellow onion in place
of green onions. Stir-fry in 1 tablespoon hot oil
and a pinch of salt until limp, 1 to 2 minutes.
Add to beef as directed above.

STEAMED BEEF
4 servings

1 lb. (net weight) *fresh* all lean beef such as top round, minced

1 slice peeled ginger, well minced

1 clove garlic, well minced

1/2 scant teaspoon salt   dash ground white pepper

2 tablespoons cornstarch   2 teaspoons oil

2 tablespoons oyster sauce

1 green onion, minced or chopped (optional)

Mix all ingredients, except onion, together and place in a 10" pyrex pie plate. Spread mixture to cover the bottom of dish.

Assemble steaming utensils, then bring water to the just-beginning-to-bubble stage. Place beef dish in steamer, turn heat to medium-low, and begin timing. The water should just be simmering; do not boil vigorously as beef tends to get tough. Check for doneness after 8 or 9 minutes. Total steaming time is approximately 10 minutes. Sprinkle green onion on top, remove steamer from heat, cover and keep hot until ready to serve. If the steaming water is too hot, partially uncover steamer to prevent overcooking. Serve with hot cooked rice. Be sure to use fresh meat; frozen meat usually contains excess water.

STIR-FRIED OYSTER BEEF WITH ONION
3 or 4 servings

3/4 lb. flank steak, thinly sliced (less than 1/8") across grain and marinated in:

   1-1/2 tablespoons cornstarch

   1/2 teaspoon salt

   pinch ground pepper

   1 teaspoon sesame oil

   1/2 tablespoon oil

   1/2 tablespoon *each* cream sherry and dark soy sauce

Mix:

   1/8 teaspoon sugar

   1 teaspoon cornstarch

   1 to 2 tablespoons oyster sauce

   1/2 cup beef broth

oil for cooking

2 slices peeled ginger

1 green onion, cut in 1" lengths

Set wok over high heat until hot. Add 2 tablespoons oil. When hot, add ginger; stir and press to extract flavor. Add meat; stir-fry to desired doneness, adding onion the last few seconds. Remove from wok and set aside. Pour gravy mixture into wok; cook and stir until clear. Spoon over beef; toss and serve.

TOMATO BEEF
3 or 4 servings

3/4 lb. (net weight) flank steak (top sirloin or chuck), thinly sliced against grain, marinated in:

  1/2 teaspoon beef bouillon powder (optional)

  1/2 teaspoon salt

  1/8 teaspoon ground pepper

    1 tablespoon cornstarch

  1/2 teaspoon sesame oil

  1/2 tablespoon *each* sherry and soy sauce

oil for cooking

  2 lb. fresh tomatoes, cut in wedges

  2 slices peeled fresh ginger or 2 cloves garlic, crushed

1/2 green onion, matchstick-cut

  3 to 4 teaspoons brown sugar

salt to taste (about 1/4 heaping teaspoon)

Heat wok until hot; add 1 to 2 tablespoons oil. When oil is hot, add ginger; stir to brown and extract flavor. Add beef and stir-fry to desired doneness, 1-1/2 to 2 minutes. Remove beef and set aside. Add another tablespoon oil to wok, then add tomatoes. Stir and toss until heated through and starting to boil. Add brown sugar, salt and onion. Stir then pour into server. Top with meat; gently mix. Serve over hot cooked rice.

GINGER BEEF
4 servings

1 lb. flank steak, thinly sliced against grain and marinated in:

  1-1/2 tablespoons cornstarch

      1 teaspoon *each* sesame oil & cooking oil

    1/2 teaspoon salt

    1/8 teaspoon ground pepper

      1 teaspoon *each* sherry and soy sauce

Mix:

    1/4 teaspoon sugar

      1 teaspoon cornstarch

    1/3 cup beef broth

1/4 to 1/3 cup slivered tender ginger root*

oil for cooking   more salt, if needed

Heat wok until very hot, add 2 to 3 tablespoons oil. When oil is hot, add ginger and stir until only heated through, 10 to 15 seconds. Add beef; stir-fry over high heat until almost done. Pour in cornstarch mixture and stir until thickened and the meat is tenderly cooked. Season with more salt, if desired. Serve immediately.

* If tender young ginger is not available, use the best ginger you have.

TENDER AND SUCCULENT BEEF SHIU MAI
makes 20 large walnut-sized meat balls

1 lb. (net weight) all lean chuck, top round or top sirloin, minced (preferably chopped with cleaver), mixed with:

    1 slice peeled ginger, well minced

    1 piece (size of nickel) well-aged dried tangerine peel, soaked to soften, very finely minced

  1/2 teaspoon *each* salt, sugar and baking soda

    dash ground white pepper

    2 tablespoons lard (shortening or oil may be substituted)

    2 teaspoons light soy sauce

    1 tablespoon oyster sauce

Mix:

    2 tablespoons cornstarch

    2 tablespoons water

watercress, fresh spinach or softened dried bean curd sheets

sesame oil (optional)

With hand, turn and mix meat mixture as if it were dough. Gather mixture into a giant meat ball. Pound the meat by throwing (throw hard) meat ball into mixing bowl 15 to 20 times. Then gradually add the liquid starch while mixing. Repeat "throwing" another 15 to 20 times. Divide meat into 20 parts. Roll into balls. Each meat ball will have the size of a large walnut. Place meat balls in a heatproof pie plate that has already been lined with greens or bean curd sheets.

Steam above gently simmering water until tenderly cooked, about 15 minutes. Sprinkle a little sesame oil over meat balls. Serve as dim sum, appetizers or as a meat dish for dinner.

4 servings

cooking oil, use 1 to 1-1/2 tablespoons at a time

3   thin slices fresh ginger root

1   to 2 tablespoons oyster sauce (or hot Chinese
    barbecue sauce for spicy beef)

fresh coriander for garnish

1   lb. (net weight) all lean top sirloin, cut across
    the grain into 2"x2"x1/4" thick pieces, well-
    drained (placed in refrigerator) if frozen,
    marinated for 2 hours in:

    1/8   scant teaspoon ground pepper (or a
          generous sprinkle)

    1   tablespoon cornstarch

    1/4   heaping teaspoon salt

    1   teaspoon cream sherry

    1   tablespoon Chinese barbecue sauce*

    1/2   teaspoon *each* sesame oil and cooking oil

Set wok over high heat until hot. Coat it with 1 to
2 tablespoons oil. Add 1 slice of ginger; stir
until pungent. Brown meat, 2 or 3 pieces at a time,
on both sides to desired doneness, 10 to 15 seconds
on each side, depending on personal preference and
thickness of meat. Add more oil around the sides
of wok as needed. This technique creates the
sizzling effect and imparts flavor to meat. Add
the remaining ginger, one slice at a time, some-
time during cooking to flavor the oil and hence

the beef. Remove steaks as the pieces get done. When
the cooking is done, turn heat off. Wipe off excess
oil in wok. Return meat to wok and pour oyster sauce
over meat. Quickly toss, garnish and serve. These
steak cubes melt in the mouth. Great for dim sum or
as a meat dish for dinner.

* Chinese barbecue sauce comes in various consistencies
and flavors. Generally, 2 to 3 teaspoons would be sufficient. Hoisin sauce or chee hou sauce can also be
used as a substitute, but each sauce gives a different
flavor. See Chinese barbecue sauce in INGREDIENTS.

BEEF "FRIDAY CURRY"
3 or 4 servings

3/4 lb. flank steak (top sirloin or chuck), thinly sliced (less than 1/8") across grain and marinated in:

> 1-1/2 tablespoons cornstarch
>
> 1/2 teaspoon *each* salt and sesame oil
>
> dash ground pepper
>
> 1/2 tablespoon *each* cooking oil, dark soy sauce, and sherry (or Chinese rice wine)

1/2 cup thinly sliced carrot, parboiled until crisp-tender

1 or 2 slices peeled ginger, slightly crushed

1 green onion, cut in 1" long thin strips

sesame oil (optional)

oil for cooking

Gravy: mix

> 1/8 teaspoon sugar
>
> 2 teaspoons curry powder
>
> 1/2 cup beef broth
>
> 1 teaspoon cornstarch

Set wok over high heat until hot. Add 2 tablespoons oil. When oil is hot, add ginger; stir and press to extract flavor. Add meat; stir-fry to desired doneness, adding onion the last few seconds. Remove and set aside.

Pour gravy mixture into wok and add carrot; cook and stir until thickened, then spoon over beef. Sprinkle with a little sesame oil; mix. Transfer to server and garnish with several raw onion shreds, if desired.

TENDER AND FLAVORFUL SPICY BEEF
4 servings

oil for frying

1 lb. (net weight) flank steak (top sirloin or best part of chuck may be substituted), cut lengthwise into 3 strips, then cut strips across grain into 1/4" thick pieces, marinated in:

  2 slices peeled fresh ginger, finely minced (for garlic beef, use 2 large cloves garlic, finely minced)

  1/2 scant teaspoon salt

  1 teaspoon *each* sherry, soy sauce and cooking oil

Paste: blend until smooth

  4 tablespoons cornstarch

  2 tablespoons all-purpose flour

  pinch of salt

  3-1/2 tablespoons (approximately) water

Sauce: mix together

  1 slice peeled ginger, finely minced (for garlic beef, use 1 clove garlic, finely minced)

  2 tablespoons hot Chinese barbecue sauce (or Chinese barbecue sauce and add chili oil to taste)

Add paste to marinated beef; mix well and separate the pieces.

Heat 1/2 to 3/4 cup oil in wok until very hot, about 365° F. Add 1/3 or 1/2 the meat to oil. Stir as fast as you can to separate and cook the pieces until golden and just cooked through, about 1-1/2 minutes. Spoon into strainer. Reheat oil and fry remaining beef. Pour oil into container; reserve for other uses.

Heat wok (which is well oiled after frying) until very hot. Add fried meat and quickly toss 2 or 3 times. Pour in sauce around sides of wok. Turn heat off. Again, quickly toss several times to mix. Do not overcook. Immediately spoon meat into server. Meat is tender and flavorful.

Note. Hot Chinese barbecue sauce, like Chinese barbecue sauce, comes in various consistencies and flavors. Some are very sweet and some are very spicy. Adjust the amount to your own preference.

SPICY BEEF
3 servings

3/4   lb. flank (chuck or top sirloin), thinly
       sliced across grain, marinated in:

  1/4   teaspoon salt

    2   teaspoons cornstarch

    1   teaspoon cream sherry

    2   teaspoons soy sauce

    1   teaspoon oil

oil for cooking

  2   to 4 dried red hot Japones, whole

  2   cloves garlic, minced

1/4   cup matchstick-cut peeled carrot shreds

1/4   cup sliced bamboo shoots

  1   green onion, cut in 1" thin shreds

1/2   teaspoon sugar

1/2   teaspoon sesame oil

Heat wok until very hot. Add 2 tablespoons oil.
When hot, add chili peppers; stir until darkened.
Dried peppers burn easily. Remove wok from heat
momentarily if necessary. Add garlic; stir a few
times. Turn to high heat, add beef and quickly
stir and toss to cook meat, 1-1/2 to 2 minutes.
Remove beef and set aside.

Reheat wok and add 1 tablespoon oil and a pinch of
salt. Add carrot and bamboo shoots; stir until hot
and thoroughly coated with oil. Add 2 to 4 tablespoons water (more as needed); stir to cook for
about 2 minutes or until carrot shreds are crisp-
tender and all the liquid has been absorbed. Remove wok from stove. Add green onion, sugar, sesame
oil and beef. Toss to mix. Serve at once.

Variation: Make KUNG PAO BEEF. Dissolve 1/2 tablespoon cornstarch in 1/2 cup beef broth, and have
1/3 cup dry-roasted peanuts ready. When vegetables
have reached the crisp-tender stage, add gravy;
stir until thickened. Remove wok from heat, add
green onion, sugar, sesame oil, beef and peanuts.
Toss and serve.

SZECHWAN SPICY BEEF
2 or 3 servings

3/4 lb. (net weight) flank steak, top sirloin or chuck, thinly sliced across grain, marinated in:

- 1/8 teaspoon garlic powder (or 1 clove garlic, minced)
- 1/4 teaspoon + a pinch salt
- 2 tablespoons cornstarch
- 1 tablespoon oil
- 1/2 tablespoon sherry
- 1 teaspoon thin soy sauce

Sauce: mix

- 1/2 teaspoon *each* sugar and sesame oil
- 1 teaspoon cornstarch
- 4 tablespoons beef broth

oil for cooking

1/2 cup sliced bamboo shoots or parboiled carrot slices*

1 piece (2" square or so) preserved Szechwan mustard (canned in spices--hot), slivered

1 fresh hot red chili pepper, cut into shreds

chili powder or chili oil to taste

Heat about 1/2 cup oil until hot. Add beef. Working as fast as you can, stir to separate and cook the meat until beef is almost done, 30 to 60 seconds. Pour into colander; drain oil. Reserve oil for other stir-fry dishes. (Beef can also be stir-fried in 2 to 3 tablespoons hot oil.)

Reheat wok over high heat. Add 2 to 3 teaspoons oil. Stir-fry bamboo shoots, mustard shreds and chili pepper until hot through. Add sauce; stir and bring to a boil. Turn heat off. Add beef. Quickly toss and mix. Season with chili powder and/or salt to taste, if needed. Serve immediately.

* Use a combination of bamboo shoots with red pepper *or* carrot with green pepper for colorful contrast.

RED-COOKED TONGUE
3 or 4 servings

1   3-lb. beef tongue (or leg of lamb)
Sauce:
- 1   large star anise
- 2   cloves garlic, crushed
- 3   1/8" thick slices ginger
- 1   small yellow onion, halved
- 2   to 4 dried red hot chili peppers, if desired
- 3/4 teaspoon salt
- 1   tablespoon *each* brown sugar and hoisin sauce
- 2   tablespoons *each* sherry and dark soy sauce
- 2   cups water, more if needed during cooking

Drop tongue into a large pot of boiling water. Cook
for 15 minutes. Drain. Remove the thick white covering and fat. Rinse and drain. Bring sauce to a boil.
Add tongue and continue to cook until it boils again.
Reduce to medium-low heat. Simmer until tender, 1
hour and 30 minutes to 1 hour and 45 minutes. The
sauce should be gravy-like. If sauce is too thin,
remove tongue and continue to boil sauce over higher
heat, uncovered, until a gravy consistency remains.
Skim fat and discard anise, onion and ginger. Slice
tongue, pour gravy over and serve hot. For variation, cook tongue in EVER-LASTING FLAVOR-POT SAUCE.
See page 78.

CHINESE POT ROAST
4 or 5 servings

4   to 4-1/2 lb. beef chuck pot roast (or leg of lamb),
    excess fat removed, cut meat into 4 or 5 big pieces
Sauce:
- 1/2 teaspoon Chinese 5-spice
- 2   slices ginger (size of quarter but twice
      the thickness), crushed
- 2   large cloves garlic, crushed
- 1   small onion, quartered
- 2   tablespoons sherry or Chinese rice wine
- 1   cup EVER-LASTING FLAVOR-POT SAUCE, page 78
- 2   cups water, more or less

Drop meat into a large pot of boiling water and bring
to a boil. Drain and rinse meat under cold running
water to remove foam. (Or, heat 2 cups oil until hot.
Add meat. Fry until all sides are brown. Drain.
Discard oil.)

Bring sauce to a boil, then add meat, and bring to a
second boil. Reduce heat to medium-low and simmer
until meat is tender, 1-1/4 hours to 1-1/2 hours,
depending on your cookware. Lift meat out of sauce.
Skim oil. If there is too much sauce, boil over high
heat, uncovered, until the desired consistency is
obtained. Return meat to sauce. Serve.

MONGOLIAN BEEF
3 servings

3/4 lb. (net weight) flank steak (chuck, top round or top sirloin), thinly sliced across the grain, marinated in:

- 1/2 scant teaspoon salt
- 2 tablespoons cornstarch
- 1 tablespoon oil
- 1 teaspoon sesame oil
- 1/8 scant teaspoon ground pepper
- 1/2 tablespoon sherry

Sauce: mix

- 3/4 teaspoon sugar
- 1 tablespoon dark soy sauce
- 2 tablespoons beef broth or water
- 1 tablespoon salted black beans, soaked, rinsed and mashed

oil for cooking

- 2 cloves garlic, minced
- 2 to 5 dried red hot chili peppers, seeded, crushed; see dried red hot chili pepper in INGREDIENTS
- 2 or 3 green onions, cut in thin shreds 1-1/2" long
- 1/2 oz. vermicelli (bean threads), deep-fried; see rice sticks in CHICKEN SALAD WITH GARLIC-SOY DRESSING for reference

toasted white sesame seeds, see sesame seeds in INGREDIENTS

Heat wok until hot. Add about 1/2 cup oil. When oil is moderately hot, add beef. Stir to separate and cook the pieces until just tenderly done. Spoon beef with oil into strainer to drain the oil. Reserve oil for other uses.

Reheat wok over medium-low heat. Coat it with 2 to 3 teaspoons oil. Add dried peppers; stir until peppers just turn brown. Add garlic and stir several times or until garlic is golden. Add sauce; stir and cook to a boil. Turn heat off. Add beef and most of the onion shreds. Quickly toss to mix.

Spoon beef into server which has been lined with fried vermicelli, sprinkle sesame seeds over top of meat, and garnish with remaining raw onion shreds.

Variation: Substitute lamb for beef and proceed as directed.

RED-COOKED BEEF STEW
2 or 3 servings

2-1/2 to 3 lb. (or 2-1/4 lb. net) boneless chuck, cut in chunks, marinated in:

    2 tablespoons cornstarch

    1 tablespoon Chinese rice wine or dry sherry

2 slices peeled ginger

1 star anise

1 or 2 dried hot chilies (such as Japones), whole

1 piece (1-1/2" square) dried tangerine peel

1 whole green onion, dip in boiling water then tie into a knot; or use 1 stalk outer tough piece of celery, cut in 3" lengths

1/4 cup dark soy sauce

1 tablespoon firmly-packed brown sugar

1 teaspoon sesame oil

1 cup water, add more as needed

stir-fried greens, such as bok choy, asparagus, snow peas, spinach or green Swiss chard to line platter

oil for deep-frying

Deep-fry marinated beef chunks (or brown meat in a wok with 1/4 cup oil) until golden. Drain oil.

Place all ingredients, except sesame oil and greens, in a heavy-bottomed pot. Bring to a boil, then reduce heat to medium-low to maintain a strong simmer. Cover and cook until tender, about 1-1/2 hours. There should be a small amount of thick sauce. Skim out fat and add sesame oil.

Line a serving platter with stir-fried greens, then top with stewed beef. Serve hot with or without rice or noodles.

Variation #1: Add 1 lb. peeled turnip chunks (Chinese, Japanese or regular variety) to pot during the last 20 minutes of cooking and cook until the turnips are moist and plump and the meat is tender.

Variation #2: Omit dried hot chilies. Add 3 to 4 teaspoons of curry powder during the last 15 minutes of cooking.

MONGOLIAN LAMB
3 servings

3/4 lb. (net weight) all lean lamb (from loin or leg; 2 lb. leg yields 1 lb. lean meat), thinly sliced across grain and marinated for 30-60 minutes in:

- 2 tablespoons cornstarch
- 1/2 scant teaspoon salt
- 1/8 teaspoon ground black pepper
- 2 slices peeled ginger, well minced
- 1 tablespoon cooking oil
- 1 teaspoon sesame oil

Sauce: mix

- 3/4 to 1 teaspoon sugar
- 1 tablespoon *each* dark soy sauce and Chinese rice wine (or sherry)
- 1 teaspoon sesame oil
- 2 teaspoons hoisin sauce
- 1/2 teaspoon rice vinegar (optional, for a subtle taste)
- 2 tablespoons beef stock or water

1 yellow, red or white onion, cut into thin slices (or 1/2 oz. vermicelli, deep-fried)

2 to 5 dried hot chili peppers, seeded, crushed; see dried red hot chili pepper in INGREDIENTS

2 large cloves garlic, crushed and chopped

2 green onions, cut into 1-1/2" thin strips

toasted white sesame seeds (optional), see sesame seeds in INGREDIENTS

Stir-fry onion slices in 2 tablespoons hot oil with a pinch of salt until wilted but still crisp, 1 to 1-1/2 minutes. Remove with slotted spoon, leaving oil in wok.

Add about 1/2 cup oil to wok and heat until very hot. Add lamb and quickly stir to separate and cook the pieces just until the color changes but the meat is still not quite cooked through, 30 to 60 seconds. Stir as fast as you can; do not overcook. Pour into strainer. Reserve oil for other uses.

Reheat wok. Coat it with 2 to 3 teaspoons (or as little as possible) oil. Add dried peppers; stir until brown. Add garlic and stir several times. Add lamb; quickly stir once or twice. Sizzle sauce over meat around the sides of wok and add most of the green onion. Turn heat off. As quickly as you can, toss several times to mix.

Spoon lamb onto server which has been lined with fried onion (or fried vermicelli), sprinkle sesame seeds on top of meat, and garnish with remaining green onion shreds.

POULTRY

CRISP TANGY LEMON CHICKEN
3 servings

oil for deep-frying

1-3/4 lb. (6 pieces) chicken thigh

Marinade: add to chicken, see below

    1/4 teaspoon salt

    1/8 scant teaspoon ground pepper

    1 teaspoon cornstarch

    1 teaspoon *each* sherry and thin soy
      sauce

Batter: mix

    4 tablespoons cornstarch

    2 tablespoons all-purpose flour

    a pinch *each* of salt and pepper

3-1/2 tablespoons water

    1/2 teaspoon thin soy sauce

Sauce:

    1/2 heaping teaspoon cornstarch

    1/3 cup chicken broth

    3 tablespoons lemon sauce, see lemon sauce
      in INGREDIENTS

    1/2 teaspoon sesame oil or cooking oil

On the meat side of the thigh, cut a slit along and over the bone. Then cut around the bone and remove bone, leaving skin and meat all in one piece. Scrape off excess fat and discard blood vessels. Marinate chicken for 2 hours or overnight in refrigerator.

Roll each piece lengthwise into a "jelly roll" with the skin wrapping the outer surface. Secure with a short skewer or toothpick. Evenly coat chicken with batter.

Deep-fry thighs in 365° F. oil until golden brown and cooked through, 8 to 10 minutes, depending on the size. Drain on absorbent toweling, then transfer to serving platter.

In a small saucepan, mix cornstarch and broth. Stir and cook until thickened. Add lemon sauce and sesame oil. Pour over chicken here and there, or serve the sauce on the side for dipping.

CRUNCHY TENDER CHICKEN
4 servings

1   3 to 3-1/4 lb. chicken, rinsed, pat dry

2   tablespoons cornstarch mixed with 2 tablespoons
    all-purpose flour

oil for deep-frying

garnish, see FANCY GARNISHES

Marinade: mix together

    1   teaspoon Chinese 5-spice

    1   teaspoon salt

  1/2   teaspoon ground ginger

    2   tablespoons Szechwan hot bean sauce,
       well-mashed*

Rub marinade over chicken, inside and out. Leave chicken in refrigerator overnight.

Set chicken on a 10" pyrex pie plate and steam over medium to medium-high heat for 1-1/2 hours; replenish steamer with boiling water as needed. Remove chicken to rack to drain and cool. Reserve stock for other uses. When cooled, pat chicken cavity dry and remove any excess sauce left on the skin. Dust flour mixture all over chicken. Set aside for 10 minutes.

Deep-fry chicken in 375° F. oil until all sides are crisp brown, 4 to 5 minutes. Chicken is very tender and crunchy; lift it out of oil with care. Drain chicken on rack. Garnish and serve whole or cut-up. Tangy lemon sauce will make an excellent dipping sauce for this chicken. See CRISP TANGY LEMON CHICKEN for reference.

* Szechwan hot bean sauce, by itself, is hot and spicy; this dish is not. Steaming the chicken for an hour and a half reduces the spiciness to a pleasant fragrance.

STIR-FRIED CHICKEN IN WINE SAUCE
3 or 4 servings

oil for cooking

1 small carrot, peeled, sliced thinly, parboiled
   2 to 3 minutes or until just crisp-tender

4 large fresh mushrooms, sliced

1 green onion, cut in 1" lengths

chicken broth (or water) for sprinkling

1-1/2 lb. chicken breast, skinned, boned, diced,
       marinated in:

    1 clove garlic, finely minced (or a
       generous dash of garlic powder)

  1/2 teaspoon salt

    1 tablespoon cornstarch

    1 teaspoon *each* thin soy sauce and
       sesame oil

    1 to 2 tablespoons chicken broth (add
       this to chicken and mix well just
       before cooking)

Sauce: mix

    1 teaspoon cornstarch

  1/2 to 1 teaspoon sugar or to taste

    2 tablespoons sherry

    6 tablespoons chicken broth

Heat wok until hot. Add 2 to 3 teaspoons oil and a pinch of salt; stir a few times. Add carrot and mushrooms; stir-fry only until crisp-tender, 1-1/2 to 2 minutes. Sprinkle 1 to 2 tablespoons chicken broth or water over vegetables during cooking. Remove and set aside.

Wipe wok with a dampened towel. Reheat until very hot. Add 1-1/2 to 2 tablespoons oil. When hot, add chicken. Stir and toss until almost cooked through. Give sauce a thorough stir, then pour over chicken around the sides of wok. Stir and toss until thickened and bubbly. Turn heat off. Add cooked vegetables and onion. Mix. Total cooking time for chicken takes 3 to 4 minutes. Serve with hot cooked rice or noodles.

DRUMSTICKS SIMMERED IN GARLIC SAUCE
4 to 6 servings

  2   tablespoons oil
1/2   teaspoon salt
  2   slices ginger, crushed
 10   cloves garlic, crushed
 12   large chicken drumsticks
  2   tablespoons sherry
  4   tablespoons dark soy sauce
  6   to 8 whole cloves
  2   cups water
  1   green onion, chopped

Heat wok until hot. Add oil, salt, ginger and garlic. Stir several times. Add drumsticks; stir and turn to sear until golden brown spots appear here and there. Sizzle sherry and soy sauce over chicken. Mix well, then add whole cloves and water. Cover and simmer over medium heat for about 30 minutes. If there is too much liquid, uncover, and cook over high heat until a gravy consistency remains. Skim fat, shower in onion, toss and serve.

CHICKEN WITH CORN AND PEPPER
4 or 5 servings

  1   recipe LOW-CAL CHICKEN MEAT, cooked in water until almost done as directed, page 73
  1   or 2 cloves garlic, crushed
  1   red bell pepper, seeded, sliced
  4   oz. (1/2 can) baby whole corn (cut in half)
  1   green onion, chopped
salt and ground pepper   oil for cooking
Sauce: mix
     1-1/2   teaspoons cornstarch
        1   teaspoon *each* thin soy sauce and sherry
      3/4   cup chicken broth

Heat wok until hot. Add 1 to 2 teaspoons oil and a pinch of salt. Stir-fry bell pepper and corn until crisp-tender, 1 to 2 minutes. Sprinkle 1 to 2 table-spoons of water over vegetables whenever wok gets dry and as needed. Spoon into a dish and set aside.

Reheat wok and add 2 to 3 teaspoons of oil. Brown garlic to extract flavor. Add chicken and quickly toss several times. Pour in sauce around sides of wok and add green onion; stir and cook until sauce is thickened. Turn heat off. Mix in vegetables; season with more salt and/or ground pepper, if desired. This is a wonderful dish for dieters.

HOT AND SPICY STIR-FRIED CHICKEN
3 servings

oil for cooking

1   clove garlic, crushed

1   fresh green hot chili pepper, seeded, cut
    into slivers

1   fresh red hot chili pepper, seeded, cut into
    slivers

1/3   cup sliced bamboo shoots

1-1/2   lb. chicken breast, skinned, boned, thinly
        sliced across the grain, marinated in:

  1/2   teaspoon *each* chicken bouillon powder
        (optional) and salt

  1   tablespoon cornstarch

  2   teaspoons sherry or Chinese rice wine

  1/2   tablespoon *each* soy sauce and cooking oil

  1   to 2 tablespoons chicken broth (add this
      to meat just before cooking and mix
      well; meat won't stick together)

Gravy: mix

  1   teaspoon sugar (more or less to taste)

  1/8   teaspoon salt

  1   teaspoon *each* cornstarch and soy sauce

  1/3   cup chicken broth

Heat Wok. Add 1 to 2 teaspoons oil. When hot, add
green and red peppers and bamboo shoots. Stir-fry
for about 2 minutes, sprinkling 1 to 2 tablespoons
of water over vegetables as needed. Season with
a pinch of salt. Remove and set aside.

Reheat wok; add 2 tablespoons oil. Brown garlic,
then add chicken and stir-fry until almost tenderly
cooked, 2 to 2-1/2 minutes. Add sauce mixture;
stir until thickened. Return vegetables to wok;
toss. Serve with hot cooked rice or noodles.

CHICKEN WITH HAM IN EGG SAUCE
4 servings

1   recipe LOW-CAL CHICKEN MEAT, cooked in water
    until almost done, see page 73

1   cup fresh or frozen (thawed) green peas

1   slice ginger, crushed

1   clove garlic, crushed

2   egg whites, beaten to a light froth with
    2 tablespoons water

1/4   cup chopped cooked ham

1/2   teaspoon sesame oil

oil for cooking

Sauce: mix

   1   teaspoon cornstarch

   1/4   teaspoon sugar

   1   teaspoon sherry

   3/4   cup chicken broth

Heat wok until hot. Add 2 teaspoons oil and 1/8
teaspoon salt; stir around a few times. Add peas
and stir-fry until just tender, sprinkling 1 to 2
tablespoons of water over peas to sizzle and create
steam. Remove and set aside.

Clean wok, then reheat it over high heat. Add 2
to 3 teaspoons oil, ginger and garlic; stir and press
to extract flavors. Add chicken and quickly toss to
mix with seasoning. Give sauce mixture a thorough
stir and add to chicken around sides of wok. Stir
until thickened. Turn heat low (gas stove) or off
(electric stove). Pour egg white over chicken.
Gently fold several times. Add ham, sesame oil and
peas; fold again. Total cooking time for this part
takes 2 to 2-1/2 minutes.

Variations: Substitute 1 cup cooked and flaked
crab meat for chicken; or, use stir-fried or deep-
fried prawns, see HOT AND SPICY STIR-FRIED PRAWNS.

LOW-CAL CHICKEN MEAT
(to be added to other dishes)

1-1/2 lb. chicken breast, skinned, boned, thinly sliced (less than 1/8" thick) across grain, marinated in:

  1 tablespoon cornstarch

  1/2 teaspoon salt

  1 teaspoon *each* sherry and thin soy sauce

  1 egg white (just before cooking, add this to meat, mix well and separate the pieces)

oil or water for cooking

To cook in water (low-cal): In a medium-sized saucepan, bring 2 to 3 cups water to a boil. Turn heat off (electric stove) or turn to low heat (gas stove). Add chicken to boiling water; gently stir to separate and cook the pieces until chicken turns white and is just cooked through (or almost cooked through for some recipes), 1 to 1-1/2 minutes. Pour into strainer. Reserve liquid for stock.

To cook in oil: Heat wok until hot. Add 2 to 3 teaspoons oil and heat until very hot. Add chicken. Quickly stir and toss to cook the meat, 2 to 3 minutes.

GAI DING IN HOT SAUCE
4 servings

1 recipe LOW-CAL CHICKEN MEAT, cooked in water until just cooked through, see recipe on left

2 dried red hot chili peppers, seeded, crushed (omit if you do not desire a hot and spicy dish)

2 cloves garlic, minced

1 green onion, cut in thin shreds

oil for cooking

Sauce: mix

  1/2 teaspoon cornstarch

  1/2 teaspoon sugar (may be omitted)

  1 tablespoon sherry

  2 tablespoons sweet bean sauce

  1/3 cup chicken broth

Heat wok until hot. Add 2 to 3 teaspoons oil and heat until moderately hot. Add crushed peppers; stir only to brown. Quickly add garlic and stir several times. Pour sauce around sides of wok, add chicken, and cook to a fast boil. Turn heat off. Add most of the onion shreds; toss and mix to blend flavors. Garnish with remaining onion shreds. Serve with hot cooked rice or noodles.

Note. See dried red hot chili pepper in INGREDIENTS for reference.

CURRIED CHICKEN WITH VEGETABLES
3 or 4 servings

oil for cooking

1 small carrot, peeled, sliced diagonally to less than 1/8" thick

2 cups cauliflower, cut in small flowerettes

6 tablespoons water, more or less as needed

1 cup sliced tender celery

2 slices peeled ginger, crushed

1 heaping teaspoon curry powder

1 green onion, cut in thin shreds 1" long

1 lb. chicken breast, skinned, boned, diced, marinated in:

    1 tablespoon cornstarch

    1/8 scant teaspoon ground pepper

    1/4 heaping teaspoon salt

    1 teaspoon *each* sherry, thin soy sauce and cooking oil

    1 tablespoon chicken broth or water (just before cooking, add this liquid to meat and mix well; this eliminates sticking)

Sauce: mix

    2 teaspoons cornstarch

    1/4 teaspoon sugar

    1 teaspoon sherry

    3/4 cup chicken broth

Set wok over high heat until hot. Add 2 teaspoons oil and 1/4 teaspoon salt. Stir to coat wok. Add carrot and cauliflower, stir to mix with seasoning, then add water. Cover and cook for 2 minutes. Uncover, mix in celery, stir and toss for 1 minute. There should be little or no liquid. Spoon into a dish. Set aside.

Clean and reheat wok. Drizzle 1 to 2 tablespoons oil around sides of wok. Drop in ginger and press to brown and extract flavor. Sprinkle curry powder over oil, quickly stir a few times and immediately add chicken. Stir and toss until chicken is almost cooked through, about 2 minutes. Pour sauce around chicken. Toss until thickened. Add green onion and cooked vegetables. Mix well. Serve with rice.

STUFFED BONELESS DRUMSTICKS
3 or 4 servings

6 large (1-1/2 lb.) chicken drumsticks

1 recipe EVER-LASTING FLAVOR-POT SAUCE, page 78

cooked ham or char shiu (see CANTONESE ROASTED
   PORK), cut in small sticks

coriander sprigs

oil for deep-frying

garnish of choice, see FANCY GARNISHES

Batter: mix

> 1/4 cup tempura batter mix
>
> 2 tablespoons + 1 teaspoon (approximately)
>   cold water
>
> pinch *each* of salt and ground pepper

Bring flavor-pot sauce to a boil. Meanwhile, scald drumsticks in boiling water for about 2 minutes. Swish drumsticks in boiling water to remove foam, etc. Pick out drumsticks and add to sauce, then simmer over low heat for 20 minutes or until just tender but still with their firm shape. Remove from heat and let drumsticks steep for 15 minutes to improve flavor. Pick out drumsticks. Cool.

Hold drumstick with one hand at each end. Insert thumb between meat and bone at the big end to separate meat from bone as far down as possible. Hold-ing meaty portion in palm of one hand, and with the other hand holding the bony end, gently twist (with the hand at the bony end) the bone back and forth until the bone twists around freely. Pull bone out through the big end, thus creating a long cavity. Fully stuff cavity with ham sticks and some coriander sprigs. See photo on page 89.

Coat stuffed drumsticks with batter. Deep-fry in 365° F. oil only until golden brown. Serve drumsticks whole; or, cool until very firm, then slice (knife must be very sharp) and attractively arrange the pieces in rows on platter--in an overlapping coin fashion. (This is called "gold coin chicken".)

Variation #1: Coat stuffed drumsticks in mixture of 1/4 cup corn flake crumbs and a pinch each of salt and ground pepper. Broil (third rack from broiler) until drumsticks begin to sizzle and a few golden brown spots appear here and there, about 10 minutes.

Variation #2: Do not coat, fry or broil stuffed drumsticks. Make a thin gravy with a little corn-starch and flavor-pot sauce. Add stuffed drumsticks to cooked gravy and simmer for 5 minutes.

SIMPLE-N-GOOD ROASTED CHICKEN
4 servings

1 3-1/2 lb. fryer, well-rinsed, drained, marinated overnight in:

- 1/4 teaspoon poultry seasoning
- 2 cloves garlic, minced
- 1 slice ginger, minced
- 3/4 teaspoon salt
- 2 tablespoons hoisin sauce or subgum sauce (will give different flavors)
- 1 tablespoon *each* dark soy sauce and sherry
- 1 teaspoon sesame oil

Fill a roasting pan (not too big, not too small) with just enough water to cover the bottom. Place chicken, breast side down, in pan. Pour marinade over chicken. Roast at 375° to 400° F. until the back is crisp brown, about 35 minutes. Occasionally baste chicken with drippings if you wish. Lift chicken up, place a low rack in pan, then lay chicken on rack with the breast side up, and continue to roast until done, another 20 to 30 minutes. Chicken is done if the expelled juice runs clear when a chopstick is inserted into the thickest part of the thigh. Add more water to pan if it gets dry.

Cool chicken. Skim fat from drippings. Chop chicken and serve with drippings. For those who cook for one or two, reserve the breast and 1/4 cup drippings to make SHREDDED CHICKEN WITH GARLIC SAUCE for another meal.

CHICKEN IN BLACK BEAN SAUCE
3 servings

8   chicken wings, cut at joints, reserve tips
    for stock (or 1-1/2 lb. spareribs, cut)

1   slice ginger

1   or 2 cloves garlic, minced

1/4 teaspoon salt

1   tablespoon salted black beans, rinsed, mashed

1   tablespoon *each* sherry and dark soy sauce

1/2 cup water, more if needed

1/2 teaspoon sugar

1   green onion, chopped

oil for cooking

Heat wok or a heavy-bottomed saucepan until hot.
Add 1 tablespoon oil and ginger; brown to extract
flavor. Add salt, garlic and beans. Stir a few
times. Add chicken; stir and toss for about 3
minutes. Sizzle sherry and soy sauce over chicken
and continue to stir and toss until well mixed.
Add water and sugar, cover, and simmer over medium-
low heat for 20 minutes or until tender. There
should be just the right amount of sauce. Add a
little more water if needed. Skim fat. Add half
the green onion; mix. Spoon chicken and sauce
into server. Top with remaining onion.

SHREDDED CHICKEN WITH GARLIC SAUCE
2 or 3 servings

1   whole roasted chicken breast, skinned, boned and
    shredded

Garlic Sauce:

1   to 2 teaspoons oil

4   large cloves garlic, minced

1   green onion, chopped or cut in shreds

salt and pepper to taste

mix:

1   teaspoon cornstarch

1   tablespoon water

1/4 cup *each* water and reserved
     drippings, see SIMPLE-N-GOOD
     ROASTED CHICKEN, page 76

Heat a small heavy-bottomed saucepan until hot. Add
oil; tilt pan to coat the bottom. Add garlic and
stir until lightly golden. Pour in cornstarch mixture and stir until thickened. Add salt, pepper
and half the green onion. Pour sauce over chicken
and top with remaining onion.

At the table, gently toss then serve. This is a
wonderful low-calorie dish.

EVER-LASTING FLAVOR-POT SAUCE
for cooking meat and poultry

3   tablespoons brown sugar

2   star anise (dried hot chili, cinnamon stick, Szechwan peppercorns, Chinese 5-spice or dried tangerine peel can be substituted)

4   cloves garlic (or ginger), crushed

1   green onion (or 1 stalk celery)

1/4 cup rice wine or sherry

3/4 cup *each* thin soy sauce and dark soy sauce

2   tablespoons sweet bean sauce (hoisin sauce, ground bean sauce or fermented wet bean curd can be substituted, but each sauce will yield a different flavor)

2-1/2 cups *each* stock (such as chicken broth) and water

Combine all ingredients in a heavy-bottomed saucepan. Bring to a boil. Watch it; soy sauce mixture boils over easily. Reduce heat and simmer for 30 to 45 minutes. The sauce is now ready to cook chicken, game hens, pork, duck, gizzards, beef, tongue or lamb. After each use, strain sauce and store in refrigerator or freezer. (Don't worry, a half-gallon milk carton will hold all the sauce with room to spare.) Before each use, skim fat and add more salt, spices, herbs, sugar, soy sauce or whatever ingredient is needed. It is interesting to note that the sauce improves its flavor as it ages, and the flavor-potted meat takes on a different flavor each time. Keep a separate pot of sauce for meats having a strong or distinctive odor such as lamb. Meat should be browned in oil, or scalded in boiling water and rinsed under cold running water to remove foam before flavor-potting. Add meat to boiling hot sauce, bring to a boil, reduce heat and simmer until tender (for pork, beef, duck, gizzards, tongue or lamb) or just tenderly cooked through (for chicken). Flavor-potted meat is ideal for cold-cuts. The sauce can also be used to make gravy.

It is best to select a "just-the-right-size" deep saucepan so that the sauce will cover or almost cover the chicken or meat. For reference and other ideas, see FLAVOR-POTTED CHICKEN and CHINESE POT ROAST.

In China, there is an amusing anecdote (and only an amusing anecdote) that So and So's place serves the most delicious flavor-potted food because their sauce is three generations old!

FLAVOR-POTTED CHICKEN
3 or 4 servings

1   3 to 3-1/2 lb. chicken, rinsed
1   recipe EVER-LASTING FLAVOR-POT SAUCE, page 78

While boiling flavor-pot sauce, scald chicken in a large pot of boiling water for about 3 minutes. Swish chicken in boiling water to remove foam. (For other meats, see EVER-LASTING FLAVOR-POT SAUCE for reference.) Lift chicken out and add to boiling flavor-pot sauce with the breast side up. Reduce to medium-low heat and cook for 3 minutes. Remove from heat. Let steep, covered, for 15 minutes. Do not peek. Lift chicken out. Bring sauce to a boil. Return chicken to sauce with breast side down. Reduce to medium-low heat and simmer for 3 minutes. Remove from heat and let steep for another 15 minutes. Test for doneness by inserting a chopstick into the thickest part of the thigh. If the expelled juice runs clear, chicken is done. If the juice runs pink, lift chicken out, bring sauce to a boil, return chicken to sauce with breast side down, cover and let steep 10 minutes. When chicken has reached the desired doneness, partially cover saucepan, and let chicken steep in sauce to improve flavor. Remove chicken from sauce; drain. Chop into bite-sized pieces and spoon some sauce over.

CHICKEN IN A PACKAGE
16 packages

    8   frying chicken drumsticks
  1/8   teaspoon Chinese 5-spice
  1/4   teaspoon *each* salt and grated fresh ginger
1-1/2   tablespoons cornstarch
    1   teaspoon *each* hoisin sauce and sherry
    1   tablespoon pineapple juice or syrup reserved from canned pineapple
   16   8" square foils for wrapping, lightly oiled on one side
oil for deep-frying

Chop meaty portion of each drumstick into 2 pieces; discard boney sticks. Rinse off bone chips and pat dry. Marinate chicken in 5-spice, salt, ginger, cornstarch, hoisin sauce, sherry and pineapple juice for 2 hours. Lay a foil on counter with a corner pointing toward you; place a piece of meat on oiled foil about 3" from this corner. Fold the corner over meat and roll foil toward opposite corner 2 to 3 times. Fold in corners from sides, and fold the last corner over to cover. Gently squeeze package to secure a tight seal. Fry in 375° F. oil 4 to 5 minutes. Chicken should be tenderly done, juicy and golden brown. Serve package hot for dim sum or as a meat dish for dinner.

CHINESE-STYLE ROASTED DUCK
4 or 5 servings

1   4-5 lb. duckling, cleaned, well-drained

2   teaspoons salt for rubbing duck

2   green onions or several coriander sprigs

1/4   cup chicken broth

more coriander for garnish

Marinade: mix

    1/4   scant teaspoon salt

    3   cloves garlic, minced

    3   slices peeled ginger, minced

    1/4   teaspoon ground star anise (grind star anise in blender) or Chinese 5-spice

    1/4   teaspoon ground pepper

    1   tablespoon *each* Chinese barbecue sauce, hoisin sauce, thin soy sauce, sherry and sesame oil

Starchy Coating:

    1   teaspoon honey

    1   cup water

    1   tablespoon white vinegar

    mix:

        1/2   teaspoon cornstarch

        1   tablespoon water

Cut wings at second joint, if desired. Rub the interior and exterior of duck with 2 teaspoons salt. Set aside to drain for 10 minutes. Meanwhile, prepare marinade. Rub marinade all over duck, inside and out. Neck and giblets can be marinated and cooked along side of duck or reserved for other uses. Leave duck in refrigerator 24 to 36 hours, spooning marinade over duck once or twice.

The morning of the day you want to roast the duck, brush marinade off duck skin and pour it into the cavity together with green onion (or coriander) and chicken broth. Sew up neck and tail cavities tightly so sauce won't run out. Carefully rinse duck (exterior only) under hot running water. Drain.

In a small saucepan, bring water and honey to a boil. Add vinegar. Stir the cornstarch mixture and add it to the saucepan; stir until clear. Keep it hot on stove. Place duck in a roasting pan. Pour hot mixture all over duck. Return coating mixture to saucepan and bring to a boil. Pour it over duck once more. Drain duck and discard coating mixture. Place duck in a drafty cool spot to dry for 4 to 6 hours.

Preheat oven to 400^0 F. Place duck, breast side up, on rack over an aluminum-foil-lined roasting pan. Fill pan with about 1/4" water. Roast at 400^0 F.

CHINESE-STYLE ROASTED DUCK
(continued)

for 15 minutes. Turn duck over, roast at 350° F. for 30 minutes or until back is crisp brown. Then turn duck with breast up again and roast at 350° F. until crackling brown (not burned), another 30 minutes or so. See GENERAL HINTS ON ROASTING.

Remove skewer or stitches; drain and reserve sauce from cavity. Chop duck into serving pieces, garnish with fresh coriander, and serve with reserved sauce.

CASHEW GAI KOW
25 to 30 pieces

1 large chicken breast, skinned, boned, cubed into 1" pieces, marinated in:

    1 slice peeled ginger, well minced

    a pinch ground pepper

  1/4 teaspoon salt

    1 tablespoon cornstarch

  1/2 teaspoon *each* sesame oil and sherry

    1 teaspoon thin soy sauce

1/4 to 1/3 cup raw cashew nut meats, well crushed

oil for deep-frying

Dredge chicken pieces in nuts, then deep-fry in moderately hot oil until cooked through. The pieces should not be brown; the meat and the nuts should have a pale golden color. Lower the temperature if necessary. High temperature will toughen the meat and burn the nuts.

Great for hors d'oeuvres.

STUFFED BONELESS WHOLE DUCK
4 servings

1   5-lb. duckling, deboned whole, page 19
2   to 3 tablespoons dark soy sauce
3   to 4 tablespoons all-purpose flour
Garlic-Ginger Mixture: mix together

    2   cloves garlic, finely minced

    2   slices peeled ginger, finely minced

    1   teaspoon salt

    1   tablespoon sherry

Stuffing:

    1   cup diced peeled carrots

  2/3   to 3/4 cup minced bamboo shoots

    4   or 5 dried Chinese mushrooms, soaked to soften, destemmed, minced

1-1/4   cups chicken broth, more if needed

  15   ready-to-eat cooked chestnut meats, chopped

    3   cups cooked barley* (see next page), or cooked glutinous rice, see FRIED SWEET RICE

    4   links (2 pairs) Chinese pork sausage or duck liver sausage, steamed for 10-15 minutes, diced finely

    2   to 3 tablespoons minced green onion

    1   tablespoon *each* thin soy sauce and oyster sauce (more or less to taste)

    1   to 2 teaspoons sesame oil

salt and ground pepper to taste

To cook stuffing: Heat wok until hot. Add 1 to 2 tablespoons oil and 1/2 teaspoon salt; stir to coat wok. Add carrots, bamboo shoots and mushrooms, and toss to mix with seasoning for 30 to 60 seconds. Add chicken broth, cover and cook until carrots are tender, 12 to 15 minutes. Mix in chestnuts during the last 5 minutes of cooking. By this time, there should not be too much liquid in wok. Uncover wok, add barley, sausage, and green onion; mix. Turn heat off. Season with soy sauce, oyster sauce, sesame oil, another 1/2 teaspoon salt (or to taste) and ground pepper. Thoroughly mix. Add more chicken broth if needed to make a moist stuffing. Set aside to cool.

Stuff the drummettes and the upper neck areas. Sew up the neck cavity. Stuff the legs and the remainder of the body. Do not stuff it to the point of bursting; leave some room for expansion during cooking. This recipe provides enough stuffing with one to two cups left over. (Serve leftover stuffing as a side dish for dinner.) Securely sew up the tail cavity. Place duck on a large shallow steaming dish. Shape and mold to best resemble its original form. Gently pat the garlic-ginger mixture all over duck skin. Steam duck above boiling water set over medium to

STUFFED BONELESS WHOLE DUCK
(continued)

medium-high heat for 1 hour, replenishing the pan
with boiling water if needed. Remove from heat.
When duck is cool enough to handle, brush off any
excess garlic-ginger mixture left on skin. Pat
duck dry. Brush with dark soy sauce, then generously dust with flour. Let rest for 5 to 10 minutes.

Heat oil to 375° F. in a large wok. Carefully lower
duck, with the help of two wok spatulas, into hot
oil. Deep-fry until all sides are nicely brown and
crisp, 5 to 6 minutes. The skin is crunchy and
fragile; handle the turning delicately. Drain duck.
Garnish and serve whole, halved, or quartered.

Variation: Brown stuffed duck on all sides in a
generous amount of oil, then simmer in chicken
broth until duck is tender, about 1-1/2 hours.
For stuffed boneless chicken, see Lonnie's chicken
cookbook.

* Rinse 3/4 cup pearl barley, then soak for 30
minutes. Cook barley in about 4 cups of water over
medium-low heat for 1 hour or until tender. Drain.
You should have 3 cups. Rumor has it that queens
and princesses drink "barley water" with a twist of
lemon to prolong youthful and beautiful complexion.

PRESSED DUCK
4 servings

 1 5-lb. duckling (cut off excess neck skin, excess
    fat, tail, and wings at second joint), cleaned,
    well-drained; pat dry
 1 tablespoon *each* salt and sherry
1/2 teaspoon ground star anise, see page 36
 2 tablespoons finely minced peeled ginger
 1 egg white (extra-large or jumbo), beaten
 2 tablespoons water chestnut powder mixed with
    2 tablespoons cornstarch
oil for deep-frying
 5 or 6 iceberg lettuce leaves, shredded
 4 to 6 tablespoons finely chopped toasted blanched
    almonds (or smoked almonds)
garnish, see FANCY GARNISHES
Sauce:
 1 teaspoon oil
 4 teaspoons cornstarch
 1 cup chicken broth, canned or homemade
 1 tablespoon *each* thin soy sauce and cream
    sherry
1/8 teaspoon ground star anise
coriander sprigs
salt to taste, if needed

Rub duck, inside and out, with mixture of salt, 1/2
teaspoon ground star anise, sherry and ginger. Leave
in refrigerator overnight. (Wings and gizzard can be

marinated and cooked along with the duck or add these parts to stockpot.)

Place duck over a steaming tray (one with holes to allow dripping) and steam above boiling water for 1-1/4 hours. Discard greasy steaming water. When duck is cool enough to handle, brush off excess anise and ginger left on skin. Cut duck in half lengthwise through the center breast and back. Place duck halves with skin side down; completely debone duck, leaving meat and skin intact. Tuck in the loose bits and pieces of meat. Press halves to evenly flatten, to break up fiber and to squash the fat under the skin. Brush both sides of each piece with egg white, then heavily dust with cornstarch and water chestnut powder. This helps to keep the loose pieces in place and to give duck a crunchy texture. Cut halves crosswise in two; duck is now quartered. Refrigerate until firm or until ready to deep-fry.

Heat oil to 375° F. With a wok spatula, carefully lower one or two pieces into hot oil with skin side down. Fry and turn until crisp brown, about 4 minutes. Drain on absorbent toweling.

Meanwhile, heat a heavy-bottomed small saucepan until hot. Add the 1 teaspoon oil; stir to coat pan. Pour in sauce mixture of cornstarch, broth, soy sauce and sherry; stir and cook until smooth and thick. Add ground star anise, a small handful of coriander, and season with more salt, if needed. Keep sauce hot.

Cut fried duck into bite-sized slices and attractively arrange on lettuce-lined platter. Pour sauce over duck and sprinkle almonds on sauce. Garnish. Serve at once.

Variations: Omit sauce. Serve crunchy fried duck with Chinese lemon sauce, sweet and sour sauce, plum sauce or spiced salt. For extra elegant dining, serve crunchy fried duck with plain steamed buns or Mandarin pancakes together with a sauce to spread on bun or pancake. Or, make CRISP PRESSED GAME HENS. Do not marinate and steam birds. Instead, simmer two game hens in flavor-potted sauce (page 78) until tender but still holding their firm shape. Cut, debone, etc. as directed above. Serve with or without sauce. This is an excellent dish to serve for two.

CRISP AND SAVORY PEKING DUCK
4 to 6 servings

1 5-lb. Long Island duckling, preferably with head
   on, well-rinsed and well-drained

white twine

2 to 3 feet plastic tubing, 1/3" diameter
   (available at hardware stores)

hoisin sauce

onion shreds or onion brushes (see FANCY GARNISHES),
   soaked in ice water

Mandarin pancakes (see REAL CRUNCHY ONION PANCAKES),
   or plain steamed buns (see SILVER-THREAD SAUSAGE
   ROLLS)

Seasonings for cavity: mix together

   1   teaspoon salt

   1/8 teaspoon ground pepper

   1/8 teaspoon ground ginger (or 2 slices
       peeled ginger, finely minced)

   1/8 teaspoon garlic powder (or 2 cloves
       garlic, finely minced)

Honey Syrup: mix

   1   tablespoon honey

   1   tablespoon sherry

   1/2 cup boiling water

At the first thought of cooking a Peking duck, invent
a device to enable you to hang the duck vertically
in center of oven for roasting. If this is not
possible, then assemble various roasting racks at
an angle so that when duck is placed on the top rack,
it is slightly above the center of the oven and hangs
in a tilted position. In either case, you should
have a foiled-lined drip pan below the duck with
enough space between duck and pan for circulation
of heat.

The day before you cook the duck: Tie a heavy-duty
string around the neck just below the head to facilitate hot water treatment and for hanging. Do not
trim wings or do any unnecessary cutting. If the oil
sack at the tail is intact, leave it on and cut it
off after roasting. Gently pull wings and legs away
from body to loosen joints, being careful not to
tear the skin. Remove and discard excess fat from
cavity and under neck skin (if possible). Give duck
a thorough but gentle massage to loosen skin from
meat; care must be taken not to puncture the skin.
In other words, the skin should be kept intact. Pat
the cavity dry, then rub with mixed seasonings. Sew
up tears or small cuts in skin with needle and white
thread, and tightly skewer lower cavity closed with
a small bamboo skewer. Run twine around both ends

of skewer to make sure opening is tightly closed. Do this part in advance and leave duck in the refrigerator overnight.

Early in the morning, about 7 a.m.: Cut a small air hole in the neck skin about 3" above the base of the neck. Insert a chopstick into the hole between the skin and meat and slide it 5" to 6" toward breast, past tip of "V" where the breast begins. Move it back and forth a few times to clear a "passage way" to the breast. Pull chopstick out. Insert 6" of plastic tubing into the "passage way". Have 2 to 3 feet of twine handy and loosely make a loop around the neck between the base of the neck and the air hole. Tightly hold left hand over this loose loop. Blow air (by mouth or use a bicycle plump) into the tube to inflate duck (even the wings and legs will puff up as if it were ready to fly away) to 1-1/2 to 2 times its original size. Duck is now taut like an inflated balloon. Close tube (mouth end) with thumb of right hand, and gently pull it out of neck while squeezing hard with left hand to prevent air leak. Tightly pull ends of string with right hand and teeth (that's right, it may be the best and only way when you are doing it by yourself!); then wind string around a few more times and tie up securely.

Bring a large pot of water to a boil. Place duck, at an angle with neck up, in sink. Repeatedly pour boiling water over every part of duck until skin acquires a dull white look. Hang duck in a cool drafty place to dry for 3 to 4 hours.

Brush duck with hot honey syrup. Hang up to dry for 2 hours. Reheat syrup and brush duck again. Hang up to dry for another 4 to 5 hours. At this stage, duck has a light waxy honey color.

Preheat oven to 400^0 F. Roast duck at 400^0 F. for 15 minutes, then roast at 350^0 F. for 40 minutes or until done. If duck is roasted on rack at an angle, roast at 400^0 F. for 10 minutes on each side, then roast at 350^0 F. for 40 minutes or until done, turning over as often as necessary to ensure that beautiful crackling brown skin. If wings or any part of duck gets brown too quickly, wrap or cover with foil.

CRISP AND SAVORY PEKING DUCK
(continued)

Be sure to remove foil during the last 10 minutes of roasting to insure crispy skin. See GENERAL HINTS ON ROASTING.

Carve off the crispy skin into serving pieces. Set aside. Cut drummettes and drumsticks at joints. Set aside. Debone the remainder, cut meat into serving pieces, and neatly arrange on center of platter. Next, place drummettes and drumsticks in their proper positions to outline the form of a whole duck. Now, place skin over meat.

To serve, dip an onion brush in hoisin sauce and spread sauce on pancake or bun, add a piece of skin, a piece or two of meat, and onion brush (or some onion shreds). Fold up and enjoy!!

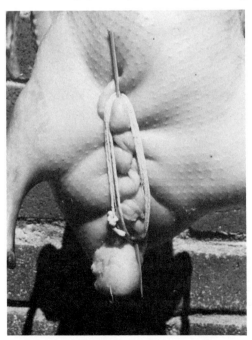

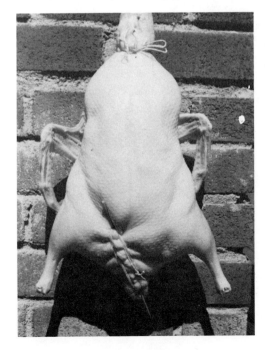

BANJO DUCK
4 to 5 servings

1 4-1/2 to 5 lb. duckling, cut off wings at second joint, cleaned, drained and dried with towel

Sauce #1:   mix

    1 clove garlic, minced

    1 slice peeled ginger, minced

  1/4 teaspoon Chinese 5-spice

  1/2 teaspoon salt

    1 tablespoon *each* Chinese barbecue sauce and hoisin sauce (or a total of 2 tablespoons chee hou sauce)

Sauce #2:

    1 cup water

    1 teaspoon honey

    1 tablespoon white vinegar

mix:

  1/2 teaspoon cornstarch

    1 tablespoon water

The day before you want to cook the duck, start working in the morning. Cut duck along the center breast. Open and flatten duck to look like a banjo. Tie a string or small wire around the neck for hanging. Skewer duck with chopsticks (or whatever you have that will work) so duck stays flat and open. Make it as flat as possible. Rub the cavity side with Sauce #1. Leave duck on a rack with the cavity side up. Set aside in a drafty place to marinate for 2 to 3 hours.

In a small saucepan, bring water and honey to a boil. Add vinegar. Stir the cornstarch mixture and add it to the saucepan; stir until clear. Keep the vinegar-honey mixture at a slow simmer. Turn duck over (after marinating for 2 to 3 hours) and tilt the rack at an angle (about 30°). Pour hot vinegar-honey over duck skin and let the mixture drip down to a pan. Pour this mixture back into the saucepan. Heat to a boil. Pour over duck skin. Repeat this for a total of four times. Hang duck in a drafty place (cold and drafty would be best; some people put a fan in front of it!). Allow the duck to drip and dry for 24 to 30 hours.

Roast duck in vertical (hanging) position, for 15 minutes at 400° F., then roast for 30 to 40 minutes at 350° F. or until done. Be sure to place a large pan, filled with a small amount of water, under duck to catch the drippings. See GENERAL HINTS ON ROASTING.

Cut off the crispy skin and place the pieces on a platter. Cut the remainder and place the pieces

BANJO DUCK
(continued)

on a second platter. Serve plain, with sweet and sour duck sauce, with thousand-layered buns, with shredded green onions, with.....anything!

Banjo duck, called *pay pah opp* in Chinese, is an excellent company or banquet specialty. It was a court dish of the Han Dynasty.

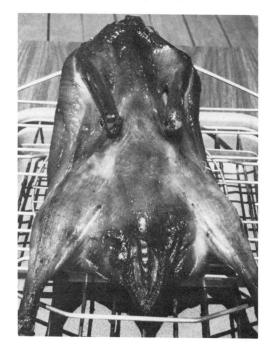

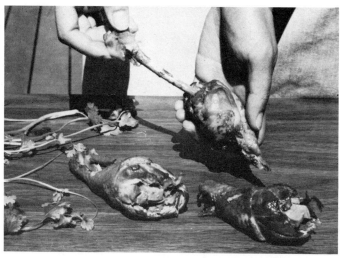

STUFFED BONELESS DRUMSTICKS, page 75

FLAVOR-POTTED CHICKEN, page 79

BRAISED SOY DUCK
4 or 5 servings

1 4-5 lb. duckling, cleaned, well-drained, cut wing tips at first joint

2 to 3 tablespoons dark soy sauce for brushing

1 green onion, chopped (or chopped coriander)

oil for deep-frying

Sauce: combine

    3 slices peeled ginger, crushed

    1 piece dried tangerine peel

    2 green onion bulbs (white parts of green onion) or 1 stalk celery (outer stalk)

    1 whole star anise

    1 tablespoon brown sugar

  1/2 teaspoon salt

    2 tablespoons sherry

  1/4 cup dark soy sauce

    3 cups water, add more boiling water during cooking if needed

Gravy: mix

    1 tablespoon cornstarch

  1/4 cup strained sauce (or water or chicken broth), see below

Pat duck dry, then air dry in a drafty place for 2 to 3 hours. This helps to keep the soy sauce on the duck skin for that beautiful red color. Brush soy sauce all over exterior of duck. Place duck in a vertical position in a drafty cool place until soy sauce is dry (or leave duck in refrigerator overnight).

Deep-fry duck in 365° F. oil until golden brown. You need not cook the duck through. Drain oil from duck. Bring sauce to a boil. Add duck, gizzard, neck and wing tips. After the contents return to a boil, reduce heat to medium-low and simmer until duck is just tender, about 1-1/4 hours. (This was done in a heavy cast aluminum pot over an electric stove. You may have to adjust the timing.) Remove duck, cool, and chop into serving pieces. Skim fat from sauce then pour through strainer. Measure one cup of sauce into pan. Bring to a boil. Add cornstarch mixture; stir until thickened. Add chopped onion. Pour over duck. Serve.

90

SEAFOOD

BUTTERFLY SHRIMP
a very special treat

1/2 lb. large prawns (about 10)

1/4 teaspoon *each* baking soda and salt

oil for deep-frying

Coating: stir to make a thick batter

    1/4 cup tempura batter mix

    pinch *each* of ground white pepper and salt

    3 tablespoons ice-cold water

Ginger Sauce:

    1 tablespoon oil

    1 tablespoon minced fresh ginger

mix:

        1 scant tablespoon cornstarch

        1/8 teaspoon salt

        1 teaspoon white vinegar

        1/2 cup water

        3 tablespoons plum sauce

Shell prawns, leaving tails intact. Slit along the back (vein side) as if slicing it in halves lengthwise, but do not cut through so it can be spread open and flattened to look twice its original size. Rinse off black veins. Drain. Mix prawns with baking soda and salt. Set aside for 30 minutes.

Meanwhile, heat a heavy-bottomed small saucepan until hot. Add 1 tablespoon oil. When oil is hot, add ginger and stir several times. Do not brown ginger. Pour in cornstarch mixture; stir and cook until translucent and bubbly. Keep hot on stove.

Rinse prawns with cold water. Drain and pat dry. Dip a prawn into batter to coat evenly. Spread open as it is lowered into 375° F. oil. Fry until both sides are golden, about 3 minutes. Fry 4 or 5 at a time for best results. Drain on absorbent toweling. Serve with ginger sauce for dip. Makes 2 to 5 servings or one person can eat it all.

To reheat, place in slow oven until hot; or, deep-fry for a second time in hot oil for 20 seconds or so.

See photo on page 30.

HOT AND SPICY STIR-FRIED PRAWNS
2 or 3 servings

oil for deep-frying

1   thin slice ginger, minced or crushed

1   small clove garlic, minced

1   to 1-1/2 teaspoons (depending on personal preference) black bean sauce with chili

1/2 large green bell pepper, seeded, cut in bite-sized slices

1/2 large onion (yellow, white or red), cut in slices

1   green onion, chopped

1/2 lb. medium-sized prawns, shelled, deveined, halved lengthwise, marinated for at least an hour in:

    1   teaspoon cornstarch

    1/4 scant teaspoon salt

    1/2 teaspoon *each* sherry and thin soy sauce

Sauce: mix

    1/4 teaspoon sugar

    1   teaspoon cornstarch

    6   tablespoons chicken broth

    1   teaspoon sherry

Deep-fry prawns in moderately hot oil until the color has changed and they are almost done. Remove and drain oil. (Or, stir-fry prawns over medium-high heat in 2 to 3 teaspoons oil until almost done.)

Heat wok until hot. Add 2 to 3 teaspoons oil and a pinch of salt. Stir-fry pepper and onion until crisp-tender. Sprinkle 1 to 2 tablespoons water over vegetables if needed. Spoon into a dish and set aside.

Clean (if needed), then reheat wok. Add 1 to 2 teaspoons oil. When oil is moderately hot, add ginger, garlic and black bean sauce; swirl a few times. Turn heat to high. Add prawns and sauce. Quickly stir and toss until it bubbles. Turn heat off. Mix in vegetables and green onion. Serve with hot cooked rice.

Variation: Add rice vinegar to taste (about 2 teaspoons) to make hot and sour prawns.

Note. A good hot and spicy dish need not be burning hot or extra spicy; excess spice can mask the delicate flavor of the principal ingredient such as prawns.

THREE-FLAVORED PRAWNS
3 servings

1   large clove garlic, crushed and cut in 3 parts

3   very thin slices ginger, crushed

1   green onion (or equal amount of Chinese chives), cut in 1" lengths

1/2 cup sliced onion, stir-fried for 1 to 1-1/2 minutes in 1 to 2 teaspoons oil and a pinch of salt; sprinkle 2 to 3 teaspoons of water over onion if wok appears dry

1/2 cup diagonally sliced celery, stir-fried for 1 to 1-1/2 minutes in 1 to 2 teaspoons oil and a pinch of salt; sprinkle 2 to 3 teaspoons water over celery if wok gets dry

1-1/2 tablespoons catsup

1/2 teaspoon curry powder

3/4 lb. medium-sized prawns, shelled, deveined, well-drained, marinated in:

   2 teaspoons cornstarch

   1/2 scant teaspoon salt

   1 teaspoon *each* thin soy sauce and sherry

Sauce: mix

   3/4 teaspoon sugar

   1 tablespoon cornstarch

   1 teaspoon thin soy sauce

   1/2 teaspoon *each* sherry and sesame oil

   1/2 cup *each* chicken broth and water

Heat 3/4 to 1 cup oil in wok until moderately hot. Scatter in prawns. Gently and swiftly stir to mix and fry until the color changes and the prawns are almost cooked through, 1 to 1-1/2 minutes. Pour prawns and oil into strainer. Save oil for cooking. Reheat wok. Separately stir-fry celery and onion as directed above. Set aside in individual bowls.

Clean wok, then reheat until hot. Add 1 to 2 tablespoons oil. When hot, add 2 slices ginger and 2 pieces garlic. Press and stir to extract flavors. Add 2/3 of fried prawns to wok; stir 4 or 5 times. Give sauce a thorough stir and pour 2/3 of it into wok; stir and cook until bubbly and thickened. Remove half of prawns with sauce to a bowl. Set aside. Add green onion to wok. Toss a few times and spoon onto serving platter to cover 1/3 of platter in a pizza-wedge fashion. Return the second half of prawns with sauce to wok. Add stir-fried onion and catsup. Toss, then spoon over same platter in wedge to cover another 1/3 of platter. Clean wok. Reheat and add 1 to 2 teaspoons of oil and remaining ginger and garlic; press and brown herbs. Add remaining fried prawns and curry powder; quickly toss several times. Pour in remaining sauce, stir and cook to a rapid boil. Mix in celery. Spoon into the remaining 1/3 of platter. Elegant and scrumptious!

MINI CRAB BURGERS
makes 14 patties

oil for cooking

1 cup flaked cooked crab meat, carefully picked over, mixed with:

    2 tablespoons all-purpose flour

    1/4 teaspoon *each* baking powder and salt

    1/8 teaspoon paprika

    1 egg, slightly beaten

    2 tablespoons *each* minced green onion and minced water chestnuts

    1 tablespoon fish sauce (or thin soy sauce)

    1 teaspoon lemon juice

    1/2 teaspoon sesame oil

Sauce: mix

    1/2 teaspoon *each* cornstarch and oil

    1 teaspoon prepared mustard

    3 tablespoons chicken broth

Heat then coat wok with 2 tablespoons oil. Spoon crab mixture into wok, using one tablespoon for each mini burger. Fry over medium-low heat for 1 minute, then turn over and flatten to form patties. Turn frequently and cook until golden brown. Total cooking time is about 4 minutes. Remove patties to platter. Pour sauce into wok; cook until thickened. Pour over patties and serve hot.

COCKTAIL SHRIMP
an excellent hors d'oeuvre

1 to 2 tablespoons oil

2 thin slices peeled fresh ginger (or 2 cloves crushed garlic, or 1 slice ginger and 1 clove garlic)

1/8 teaspoon salt

1/2 lb. medium-sized prawns, shelled, deveined, cut lengthwise in halves

1 green onion, cut in 1" lengths

Blend:

    1/2 teaspoon *each* sugar, cornstarch and brandy

    1 teaspoon dark soy sauce

    1 tablespoon water

Heat wok, then add oil. When hot, add ginger and brown to extract flavor. Add salt and prawns; stir-fry until cooked, 2 to 3 minutes. Add cornstarch mixture and stir until thickened. Toss in green onion and serve hot on platter or spear with cocktail picks and serve as hors d'oeuvres.

CRAB FU YUNG
4 servings

1/2   cup petite-sized peas, thaw if frozen

3   fresh mushrooms, coarsely chopped

4   to 6 oz. crab meat, coarsely flaked

6   eggs, beaten

1/2   teaspoon *each* salt and freeze-dried cilantro (dried and crushed coriander leaves in spice jar)

1/8   teaspoon ground pepper

2   teaspoons *each* sherry and thin soy sauce

1   teaspoon sesame oil

oil for cooking

Stir-fry peas and mushrooms together in 1 to 2 teaspoons oil only until cooked through, 1 to 1-1/2 minutes. Remove from wok and cool. Clean wok, if needed. Add peas and mushrooms to the mixture of remaining ingredients. Mix a few times.

Heat wok until hot. Drizzle 1 to 2 tablespoons of oil around wok. Pour mixture into wok. As the bottom gets cooked and begins to turn golden, lightly lift the sides of omelet and poke a few holes in the center to let the uncooked mixture run down to the bottom of the wok, but do not stir. Add more oil, 2 to 3 teaspoons at a time, around the sides of wok as needed. When the top begins to set, carefully turn the omelet over to cook to a golden brown. Lower heat if necessary. Remove omelet at once and serve. If desired, top with a little oyster sauce or soy sauce.

Crab fu yung can be served for breakfast, lunch or dinner.

STEAMED PRAWNS IN BLACK BEAN SAUCE
2 servings

1/2 lb. fresh medium-sized prawns, shelled, deveined, cut lengthwise in half

4 or 5 oz. all lean pork (such as tenderloin or pork butt roast) thinly sliced to less than 1/8" thick

1 small strip (or 1 knot) preserved salted turnip, soaked for 10 to 15 minutes

2 cloves garlic, minced

2 thin slices ginger, slivered

1 tablespoon salted black beans, soaked for 10 minutes, rinsed, mashed (see salted black beans in INGREDIENTS)

1/4 teaspoon sugar

1 tablespoon *each* cornstarch, dark soy sauce and sherry

1 teaspoon sesame oil or cooking oil

1/2 whole green onion, chopped

Cut root portion of turnip into thinnest possible slices. Use 2 tablespoons for this dish. Throw the leaf portion and any leftovers into stockpot.

Mix all ingredients, except green onion, in a heat-proof steaming plate. Scatter green onion on top. Steam above boiling water until done, about 15 minutes. Serve with rice and a stir-fried vegetable.

CRISP AROMATIC FISH
3 to 5 servings

3 small whole fish (total weight 2 to 2-1/4 lb.), cleaned and ready to cook, drained

2 or 3 slices peeled ginger, minced

2 or 3 cloves garlic, minced

1 scant teaspoon salt

all-purpose flour for sprinkling

oil for pan-frying

Mix:

   1 tablespoon sherry

   1 tablespoon thin soy sauce

Rub mixture of ginger, garlic and salt all over fish. Set aside in refrigerator for 2 to 6 hours. Then, sprinkle flour over fish on both sides. Set aside for 10 to 20 minutes.

Heat a large heavy skillet or wok until very hot. Add 2 to 3 tablespoons oil. Stir to coat the bottom well. Pan-fry fish until cooked and crisp brown on both sides. Occasionally add a little more oil around the sides of fish. This technique imparts a wonderful fried aroma to food. When fish is done, remove any excess oil in skillet. Drizzle sherry-soy over fish to let it sizzle for 10 seconds or so. Serve hot.

LOBSTER CANTONESE
2 servings

1   1-1/2 lb. *live* lobster (or 1 1-lb. *fresh* lobster tail)

2   tablespoons all-purpose flour

1   large slice fresh ginger, crushed

1   clove garlic, minced

1   tablespoon salted black beans, soaked for 10 minutes, rinsed, mashed

2   oz. boneless lean pork, minced

2   teaspoons sherry

2   teaspoons thin soy sauce

1/2   cup chicken broth or other homemade stock

1/2   green onion, chopped

1   teaspoon sesame oil

1   medium egg, beaten

water, if more liquid is needed for sauce

salt to taste

oil for cooking

Thickener: mix

    3/4   teaspoon cornstarch

    2   tablespoons water

    1/2   teaspoon sugar

With a heavy and sharp cleaver, first break off the large claws from the body, then cut off and discard the long skinny legs. Chop or break off the meaty tail from the head portion. Discard head, stomach sack and all internal matter at the large end of the lobster tail. You may save any part you wish to retain, such as the roe. For practical purposes, chop to trim off excess shell along sides of tail, and cut and discard short small legs and "thorny points" on the underside of the tail. In general, the meaty edible parts are the large claws and tail. Cut tail lengthwise in half, then chop each half crosswise into 1" chunks. To facilitate removal of shells during dining, crush claws, especially at joints, then chop each into 3 or 4 pieces. Pick out and discard any loose shells having no meat attached to them. Dredge the meat side of lobster pieces in flour. Set aside for 5 minutes while preparing other ingredients. DO NOT prepare this part in advance. Lobster must be cooked as fresh as possible.

Heat wok until hot. Add 1/2 to 1 cup oil (used oil will do fine) and ginger. When oil is moderately hot, add lobster. Stir and turn to cook lobster until meat is whitened and firm, about 1-1/2 minutes. The pieces need not be completely cooked

LOBSTER CANTONESE
(continued)

through. Pour into strainer. Reserve or discard oil.

Clean wok and reheat until very hot. Pour in 1 to 2 tablespoons oil; stir to coat wok. Add garlic and black beans, and quickly stir a few times. Add pork; stir and mix to separate the pieces until meat is just cooked through. Mix in lobster, then sprinkle sherry and soy sauce over, and give contents a thorough mix and turn. Add broth and stir again. Cover and let steam 2 to 3 minutes. Uncover, stir in thickener until cooked. Next, add green onion and sesame oil; stir and mix a few strokes. Finally, lower heat and pour beaten egg over top. Gently fold egg into contents. Season with more salt if needed. Serve with rice and stir-fried vegetables.

Note. Similarly, cook crab or prawns with this delicious sauce (commonly known as lobster sauce).

FISH TIDBITS
about 24 pieces

1/2 lb. fillet of white-meat fish (such as perch, cod, or sole), completely deboned, well-drained, cut in 1"x1"x1/4" pieces, marinated in:

> 2 thin slices peeled ginger, well minced
>
> 1/8 teaspoon salt
>
> 1 teaspoon cornstarch
>
> dash ground pepper
>
> 1/2 teaspoon *each* soy sauce, sherry and sesame oil

1 lb. bacon, cut strips in halves
5 to 7 thin slices peeled ginger, slivered finely
oil for deep-frying
toothpicks

Add one or two ginger slivers to a chunk of fish. Wrap a strip of bacon around fish. Secure with toothpick.

Deep-fry in 365° F. oil until golden brown and the bacon is slightly crisp but not dry. Drain on absorbent toweling. Serve as appetizers or party food.

SWEET AND SOUR FISH FILLET
3 servings

1 lb. perch fillet, cut into 3 to 4 inch long
   strips, marinated in:

    1/2 teaspoon salt

    1/8 teaspoon ground pepper

    2 slices peeled ginger, minced

    1 clove garlic, minced

    1 medium egg, beaten

    1 teaspoon sesame oil

Sauce: mix

    2 tablespoons brown sugar

    2 teaspoons cornstarch

    2 tablespoons white vinegar

    2 heaping tablespoons catsup

    1/4 cup water, more if needed

    1/8 teaspoon salt or to taste

cornstarch

oil for deep-frying

6 to 8 slices red bell pepper

6 to 8 slices of yellow onion

1 green onion, cut in 1" lengths or chopped

Marinate fish for about 2 hours in refrigerator.
Spread fillet over a flat surface. Sieve 1 to 2
tablespoons cornstarch over. Turn over and do the
same. Lightly work starch into fish. Let stand
for 15 minutes. Deep-fry fish in hot oil until crisp
and golden. Drain on absorbent toweling.

Heat 1-1/2 tablespoons oil in a small saucepan or
wok until very hot. Add pepper and onion slices.
Stir-fry until cooked, 1-1/2 to 2 minutes. Sprinkle
a little water over vegetables if needed. Spoon out
and set aside. Add sauce mixture to pan; stir until
thickened. Add green onion; stir and remove pan from
heat. Return pepper and onion to sauce; mix. Transfer fish to server. Spoon sauce over fish. Serve.

It is generally believed that a recipe similar to
this was originated in the palace kitchen of the
Manchu Dynasty.

Variation: Make CURRIED FISH FILLET. Replace the
above sweet and sour sauce by mixture of:

    1/4 teaspoon sugar

    2 teaspoons cornstarch

    4 teaspoons curry powder

    1/2 cup chicken broth, more if sauce is thick
        salt to taste

SWEET AND SOUR FISH
4 or 5 servings

1   2 to 2-1/2 lb. whole white-meat fish, cleaned and drained

3   slices peeled ginger root

2   or 3 cloves garlic, crushed

1/2 small yellow onion, cut in slices

1/2 red bell pepper, cut in slices (parboiled carrot slices may be substituted)

1   green onion, cut into 1" lengths

oil for cooking

additional salt

Sauce: mix

    3   tablespoons brown sugar

    1   tablespoon cornstarch

   1/4 teaspoon salt

    3   tablespoons catsup

   1/2 cup water, more if sauce is too thick

    3   tablespoons white vinegar

On both sides of the fish, make two or three diagonal slashes 2" apart, 1/4" deep for better penetration. Sprinkle fish with 2 teaspoons salt and let it stand for 1 to 2 hours in the refrigerator.

Heat 1 cup oil in wok until very hot. Add garlic and 2 slices of ginger; stir until pungent. Add fish and fry until done and crisp brown on both sides, about 15 minutes. Drain, then place on serving platter. Discard oil.

Add 1 tablespoon oil to preheated wok. When oil is hot, stir-fry yellow onion and pepper with a pinch of salt for about 1 minute. Remove and set aside.

Reheat pan with 1 tablespoon oil. Add remaining ginger; stir until brown. Add sauce and stir until thickened. Add green onion and the cooked onion and pepper. Pour sauce over fish. Serve immediately.

Note. If you wish, pour sauce around fish; fish will stay crisp longer.

STIR-FRIED FISH FILLET
3 servings

oil for cooking

3 slices peeled ginger root, lightly crushed

1/4 cup sliced bamboo shoots

4 to 6 fresh mushrooms, sliced

6 to 10 dried cloud ears, soaked until soft, destemmed, squeezed dry, (cut large "ears" into 2 pieces)

1 stalk broccoli (main stem only; save flowerettes for another dish), cut diagonally into 1/8" thick slices

1/4 cup chicken broth or water

1 lb. *fresh* fillet of perch (or any white-meat fish), completely deboned, cut lengthwise* into bite-sized thick slices, marinated for 2 to 4 hours in:

   1/2 teaspoon salt

   1 tablespoon cornstarch

   1 teaspoon *each* cream sherry, thin soy sauce and cooking oil

Sauce: mix

   1/2 teaspoon cornstarch

   1/4 teaspoon sugar

   1 teaspoon *each* cream sherry, thin soy sauce and sesame oil

   6 tablespoons chicken broth

Heat wok until very hot (almost smoking). Add 1 to 2 tablespoons oil and ginger; brown to extract ginger essence. Add fish; stir and toss until just cooked through, about 3 minutes. Spoon out and set aside. Drain oil if on low-calorie diet.

Clean wok, if needed, then reheat. (The fish will most likely not stick to a well-seasoned wok; washing and oiling again may be eliminated.) When hot, add 2 to 3 teaspoons oil and 1/8 teaspoon salt; swirl around a few times. Add broccoli, mushrooms, bamboo shoots and cloud ears. Stir and mix until well-coated with oil. Add broth or water, cover and steam until vegetables are crisp-tender, about 1-1/2 minutes. Vegetables should be almost waterless. Add sauce; stir until thickened. Turn heat off. Gently mix in fish and serve at once.

Variation: Make TOFU WITH STIR-FRIED FISH FILLET. Add stir-fried fish fillet (fish only) to cooked bean curd. See TOFU WITH SEAFOOD for reference.

* This cutting method helps to keep the pieces in shape better. It also helps in spotting and picking out the fine bones.

FISH PATTIES
16 to 20 patties

1/2 lb. fillet of white-meat fish, completely deboned

1/4 lb. boneless pork butt, not too fat and not too lean

1 slice peeled ginger, minced

pinch ground pepper

1/4 teaspoon salt

1 tablespoon cornstarch

1 teaspoon *each* sesame oil, sherry and cooking oil

1 tablespoon oyster sauce

1 egg

1 green onion, minced

1 to 1-1/2 teaspoons curry powder or Chinese chili powder, if a distinctive spicy flavor is desired

1 to 2 tablespoons chicken broth or water, if mixture is too sticky

1/2 cup dry-roasted peanuts, finely crushed until powdery

fresh coriander for garnish

oil for pan-frying

Grind or preferably chop together the fish and pork. Add ginger, pepper, salt, cornstarch, sesame oil, sherry, oil, oyster sauce, egg, green onion and curry powder (or chili powder) if desired; mix well. If mixture is too thick and sticky, add water or chicken broth and stir again.

Heat wok or a flat-bottomed skillet until hot. Coat it with oil. When oil is hot, spoon about 1-1/2 tablespoons of mixture into wok to make a mound. Cook as many mounds as you can at one time, but avoid overcrowding. Fry over medium heat for 1 minute, then turn over and flatten mounds to 2" patties and fry until both sides are delicately brown and cooked through. When pan-frying, it is best to add a little oil at a time as you fry. This helps to bring out the best flavor in food. Therefore, do not add too much oil at the beginning. Remove patties to serving platter. Sprinkle crushed peanuts on top of patties and press gently. Garnish with coriander. Serve hot.

These patties can be served as dim sum, as a seafood dish for dinner, in a sandwich, or cut into smaller pieces and served with colored toothpick for hors d'oeuvres. Great with a drink!

Instead of sprinkling crushed peanuts on patties, you may serve mustard or chili oil for dipping.

FISH WITH GROUND BEAN SAUCE
4 servings

1 whole (1-1/2 to 2 lb.) rock cod or other white-meat fish

1 green onion, coarsely minced or chopped

coriander for garnish

oil and salt

Sauce: mix

    2 tablespoons ground bean sauce or mash 2 tablespoons bean sauce

    2 or 3 cloves garlic, minced

    2 to 3 teaspoons minced peeled ginger

    1 tablespoon cream sherry

    1/2 cup water, more if needed during cooking

Sprinkle fish with 1/2 teaspoon salt. Rub. Let stand and drain for 30 minutes in refrigerator. Heat wok until hot. Coat it with 1 to 2 tablespoons oil. Pan-fry fish over medium-high heat until both sides are brown and the fish is almost cooked through, 5 to 10 minutes on each side. (While frying fish, frequently add a little oil around the sides of fish; this technique gives pan-fried food a better flavor.) Spoon out excess oil, add sauce, then cover and simmer for 10 minutes, turning fish over once. Add onion and stir into sauce. Place fish on platter; top with sauce and garnish. Serve hot.

STEAMED FISH WITH BLACK BEAN SAUCE
4 or 5 servings

1-1/2 to 2 lb. fish steaks, cleaned, well-drained

1 green onion, chopped

2 teaspoons sesame oil or chili oil for spicy fish

Sauce: mix

    1 to 1-1/4 tablespoons salted black beans, rinsed, well-mashed

    2 large cloves garlic, minced

    3 slices peeled ginger, minced

    3/4 to 1 teaspoon salt, depending on weight of fish and personal taste

    1/4 teaspoon ground black pepper

    1 tablespoon *each* sherry and oil

    1-1/2 tablespoons dark soy sauce

Place fish in a 10" pyrex pie plate. Pour sauce over both sides of fish. Leave dish in refrigerator for 2 to 4 hours. Occasionally spoon sauce over fish. Just before cooking, scatter half the chopped onion over fish. Steam above boiling water over medium-high heat until done, 15 to 25 minutes, depending on thickness of fish. Top with remaining onion and sprinkle sesame oil over. Serve hot with rice.

CURLY SQUID WITH ONION AND CHIVES
3 or 4 servings

2   lb. fresh squid (smaller squids are more desirable)

3   slices peeled ginger, crushed or slivered

2   cloves garlic, crushed

1   medium small onion, cut in slices

1   small bunch Chinese chives (or green onions), cut in 1-1/2" lengths

1/2   to 1 teaspoon sesame oil

oil for cooking

Marinade: mix

    1/4   teaspoon plus a pinch salt

    1/8   teaspoon ground white pepper

    1/2   teaspoon sesame oil

    1   teaspoon *each* oil and thin soy sauce

Sauce: mix

    1/2   teaspoon sugar

    2   teaspoons *each* cream sherry, dark soy sauce and water (or chicken stock)

Cut tentacles above the eyes; reserve for cooking. Slit body lengthwise on lighter-colored side. Remove and discard eyes, head, cartilage and all interior matter. Scrape or peel off the purple skin (membrane), if desired. Thoroughly rinse tentacles and body pieces. Drain well, then pat dry. Diagonally score the inner sides of bodies in crisscross pattern, then diagonally cut off at 1-1/2" intervals (i.e. cut small ones into 2 pieces, large ones into 3 or 4 pieces). Cut tentacles into 2 or 3 pieces if they are too large.

Add marinade to squid; mix well then set aside for at least 30 minutes.

Stir-fry onion slices in 3/4 to 1 tablespoon hot oil and a pinch of salt until almost crisp-tender, sprinkling 2 to 3 teaspoons water over onion, if needed. Add chives; stir and toss until heated through. Remove and set aside. Wipe wok clean if needed.

Reheat wok over high heat and add 1-1/2 to 2 tablespoons oil. When hot, add ginger and garlic; stir and press to slightly brown and extract flavor. Add squid. Toss and turn until the pieces begin to curl and the color changes to beige, about one minute. Cover and cook in its own juice for a minute. Un-

CURLY SQUID WITH ONION AND CHIVES
(continued)

cover, stir, turn and cook until the liquid has
evaporated and the wok begins to look dry. Sizzle
sauce around the sides of wok; stir and mix. Total
cooking time takes approximately 5 minutes. Remove
from heat. Mix in vegetables and sesame oil.
Serve at once.

Variation #1: Omit onion and/or chives and add
stir-fried squid to other stir-fried vegetables.

Variation #2: Add cooked CURLY SQUID WITH ONION
AND CHIVES to boiled bean threads.

Variation #3: For those who love hot and spicy
food, add 1 or 2 dried red hot Japones. Seed and
crush peppers. Add peppers to hot oil (in the
4th paragraph), then add ginger and garlic and
proceed as directed.

Variation #4: Add 2 teaspoons curry powder to
browned ginger and garlic, then add squid and
proceed as directed.

CURLY SQUID WITH ONION AND CHIVES, page 105

POACHED FISH, page 107

POACHED FISH
2 servings

1 *fresh* whole white-meat fish (1 to 1-1/4 lb.), scaled, cleaned and rinsed

1 slice peeled ginger, crushed

3/4 teaspoon salt, more or less

Sauce:

    3 tablespoons oil

    1 slice peeled ginger, minced

    1 clove garlic, minced

    2 dried Chinese mushrooms, soaked to soften, stems removed, sliced

    1/2 strip (or 1/2 knot) preserved salted turnip, soaked for 10 minutes, slivered

    1 tablespoon dark soy sauce

    1/4 cup chicken broth or other stock

    2 tablespoons slivered cooked ham

    1 teaspoon sesame oil

    2 or 3 sprigs fresh coriander or 1 green onion, coarsely chopped

Fill wok or a large skillet with enough water to cover fish. Add salt and crushed ginger. Turn heat on high. Cover wok with lid and bring to a full boil. Add fish; cover. Turn heat off if you are cooking over an electric stove; turn heat to lowest if you are cooking over a gas stove. Let fish steep until done, about 8 minutes. Fish is cooked if a chopstick inserts easily into the thickest part of the flesh, and the eyes pop out. Carefully lift fish out and place on platter. Discard water.

While fish is steeping and about done, heat a heavy-bottomed saucepan until very hot. Add oil. When oil is hot, remove 1 tablespoon of it for use later, then add minced ginger and garlic; stir several times to lightly brown herbs. Add mushrooms and preserved turnip; stir until heated through. Pour in mixture of soy sauce and chicken broth; cook to a boil. Turn heat off. Add ham, sesame oil and coriander. Pour sauce over *hot* fish, making sure that the entire fish is flavored with the sauce. Drizzle reserved oil over the entire dish. Garnish with additional raw coriander, if desired. Serve hot. See photo on page 106.

Note. Preserved salted turnip strips are sometimes rolled up into knots. Unroll, then proceed as directed.

STEAMED FISH
4 or 5 servings

1 1-3/4 to 2 lb. whole fish (cod, perch, sand dab or flounder); or 1 to 1-1/4 lb. fillet of cod, perch, or cod steak; cleaned and well-drained*

2 or 3 slices peeled ginger, minced

1/4 to 1/2 teaspoon salt

1/8 teaspoon ground pepper

2 teaspoons sherry

1 tablespoon dark soy sauce**

1/2 tablespoon hoisin sauce**

1 green onion, minced

1 to 2 tablespoons oil

1/2 tablespoon sesame oil

1 or 2 cloves garlic, minced

Rub fish with mixture of minced ginger, salt, pepper, sherry, soy sauce, and hoisin sauce. (Or, omit soy sauce and hoisin sauce, see below, if you desire a "clear" steamed fish.) Place fish in a steaming dish; steam above boiling water until done (7 to 8 minutes for fillet, and about 15 minutes for whole fish). Pour off excess liquid (excess only, save some for sauce), scatter onion on top, cover and keep fish piping hot.

Heat wok or a small saucepan until very hot; add oil. When oil is very hot, add garlic and sesame oil. Stir, then pour over fish. Serve immediately.

Steaming is a healthy way to cook. Low in calories. Good for those who are on a low-fat, low cholesterol diet.

* The trimmed weight of a 2-lb. whole fish is approximately 1 to 1-1/4 lb.

** You can add these sauces to fish as directed above; *or*, serve these sauces (separately or combined) on the side for dipping.

DEEP-FRIED CHOPPED OYSTERS
12 to 15 morsels

oil for deep-frying

Mix together:

   1 10-oz. jar oysters, cleaned, well-drained, coarsely chopped

   2 slices bacon, minced

   1 green onion, minced or chopped

   1 slice peeled ginger, very finely minced

   1 clove garlic, very finely minced

1/8 scant teaspoon ground pepper

1/4 teaspoon salt

   1 teaspoon hoisin sauce

   6 tablespoons all-purpose flour (add this to mixture and mix well just before cooking)

Drop mixture, a tablespoonful each, into 365° F. oil. Deep-fry until golden brown and crisp, 3 to 4 minutes. Drain on absorbent toweling. Serve hot for lunch, dinner or dim sum. Delicious!

STEAMED SAND DABS
3 or 4 low-cal servings

   1 lb. sand dabs, cleaned thoroughly, drained, marinated for 30 minutes in:

     3/4 teaspoon salt

     1/8 teaspoon ground black pepper

      1 teaspoon oil

      2 teaspoons dark soy sauce

      2 teaspoons sherry

   6 to 8 cloud ears (black fungus), soaked, destemmed, cut in half

   6 to 8 lily buds (golden needles), soaked, destemmed, cut in half

   3 or 4 dried Chinese red dates, soaked, cut in slivers

   2 or 3 slices peeled fresh ginger, slivered

   1 green onion, cut in thin shreds

   1 teaspoon sesame oil, optional

Place marinated fish, single layered, in a heatproof dish such as a large pie plate. Scatter cloud ears, lily buds, dates, ginger and half the green onion over fish. Steam above boiling water for 10 minutes. Sprinkle remaining green onion and sesame oil on top. Serve hot with rice. Be sure to pour some of this "fish sauce" over the rice. G-O-O-D !

VEGETABLES

BEEF WITH PLENTY OF VEGGIES
3 or 4 servings

oil for cooking

1 slice peeled fresh ginger

1 small carrot, peeled, cut in shreds (or 1/2 red bell pepper, cut in strips)

4 or 5 large fresh mushrooms, cut in 1/4" thick slices

1/4 cup shredded bamboo shoots

15 cloud ears, soaked to soften, stems removed, squeezed dry, cut in halves or thirds

1 large stalk broccoli, cut in 1/8" small slices (or 1 medium zucchini, cut in 1/4" thick slices)

salt, ground pepper or soy sauce to taste

1/2 cup beef broth or water

1/2 lb. (net weight) lean top sirloin, chuck or flank steak, shredded across the grain into matchstick size, marinated in:

    1 tablespoon cornstarch

    1/4 plus 1/8 teaspoon salt

    pinch ground pepper

    1/2 teaspoon *each* sherry, sesame oil and thin soy sauce

Sauce: mix

    1 teaspoon cornstarch

    1/4 cup beef broth

Heat wok until very hot. Add 1 tablespoon oil and ginger; brown to extract flavor. Add beef; stir-fry to desired doneness, about 1-1/2 minutes. Remove and set aside.

Reheat wok until very hot. Add 1 teaspoon oil and 1/4 teaspoon salt; swirl around a few times. Add all the vegetables and stir to mix with oil. Add broth or water. Cover and steam until crisp-tender, about 2 minutes. Add sauce and bring to a fast boil. Remove from heat. Mix and turn several times, then add meat. (If meat is added to boiling hot vegetables, the beef may get tough.) Season with more salt, ground pepper or soy sauce to taste. Toss and serve.

NAPA CABBAGE PEEKS THROUGH CLOUDS
a low-cal vegetarian dish

oil for cooking

1   thin slice ginger

1/2 lb. napa cabbage, cut in bite-sized pieces

4 or 5 tablespoons frozen (thawed) or fresh green peas

1/2 of an 8-oz. can straw mushrooms, drained, large ones cut lengthwise in half

salt and ground white pepper

Cloud Formation Substances:

    1 egg white, beaten

    mix:

        1   teaspoon cornstarch

        1/2 teaspoon cream sherry

        1/3 cup chicken stock

Set wok over high heat until hot. Add 2 to 3 teaspoons oil, 1/8 teaspoon salt, and ginger; stir to brown ginger. Add cabbage, peas and mushrooms. Stir and toss until well coated with oil. At this point, wok will appear dry; sprinkle 1 to 2 tablespoons water over vegetables and continue to toss and stir-fry until cabbage is limp and just cooked through, 4 to 5 minutes. Cabbage should still be crunchy. Spoon into server, leaving any liquid in wok.

Pour sauce mixture into wok; stir until thickened. Lower heat (gas stove) or turn heat off (electric stove). Slowly pour beaten egg white in a thin stream, then gently stir in a circular motion to form "clouds". Return cabbage mixture to wok. Sprinkle with a pinch of ground pepper, if desired. Gently mix 2 or 3 times. Serves 3 or 4.

CAULIFLOWER ON CLOUD EARS
3 servings

1/2 head cauliflower, cut into bite-sized flowerettes

1 medium-large carrot, peeled, diagonally cut into 1/8" thick slices (or cut with vegetable cutters for a fancier appearance)

10 cloud ears, soaked, destemmed, rinsed, drained

1/4 cup shredded cooked ham

3/4 cup water or stock

oil for cooking

salt and pepper to taste

Sauce (optional): mix

    1 teaspoon cornstarch

    1/4 cup chicken broth

Heat wok until hot. Add 1 teaspoon oil and 1/4 teaspoon salt; swirl a few times. Add carrot and cloud ears; stir until well coated with oil. Add water (or stock); cover and cook for 2 minutes. Uncover, add cauliflower, stir, then cover and cook until crisp-tender, about 3 minutes. Add sauce and stir to a boil. Add ham, pepper and more salt if needed.

See photo on page 17.

TOFU WITH SEAFOOD
3 or 4 servings

1 clove garlic, crushed

2 slices peeled ginger

1/2 lb. cooked shrimp or crab meat

1 tablespoon light soy sauce

1 teaspoon sherry

1 carton medium-firm or firm tofu, cut in bite-sized pieces

1 cup chicken broth

1 green onion, cut in 1" lengths (or coriander)

salt   ground pepper   cooking oil

Mix:

    1 tablespoon cornstarch

    1 tablespoon water

Heat 1 to 2 tablespoons oil in wok and brown ginger and garlic to extract flavors. Add seafood and stir-fry until hot. Sizzle with sherry and soy sauce. Remove and set aside. Add bean curd and broth to wok. Bring to a boil and cook for another minute. Add cornstarch mixture; stir until thickened. Add seafood, green onion, salt and pepper; give it a gentle quick stir. Serve hot with rice.

LOW-CAL CHICKEN ZUCCHINI
4 or 5 servings

 1   recipe LOW-CAL CHICKEN MEAT, cooked in
     water until just cooked through, page 73
 2   to 3 teaspoons oil
1-1/4 lb. zucchini, sliced
 1   clove garlic, crushed
 1/2 cup chicken stock, more or less as needed
salt, ground pepper, and soy sauce to taste
Mix:
       1   teaspoon cornstarch
       2   tablespoons chicken stock

Set wok over high heat until very hot. Add 2 to
3 teaspoons oil and a pinch of salt. When oil is
hot, add garlic; stir and brown to extract flavor.
Add zucchini; stir and toss until the wok appears
dry and the zucchini is thoroughly coated with the
oil. Add the 1/2 cup chicken stock. Stir and cook
until crisp-tender, about 2 minutes. Pour gravy
around sides of wok, and toss and turn until thickened. Turn heat off. Mix in chicken and season
with salt, pepper and soy sauce (if needed) to
taste.

STIR-FRIED ROMAINE LETTUCE
2 or 3 servings

 2   to 3 teaspoons oil
 1   or 2 cloves garlic, minced
 1/4 teaspoon salt (or to taste)
 4   or 5 fresh mushrooms, sliced
 1   large head of romaine lettuce, washed, drained,
     pat dry, cut in bite-sized pieces
 1/4 teaspoon sugar
 1/2 teaspoon sherry
 1/2 teaspoon thin soy sauce

Set wok over high heat until very hot. Add oil, salt
and garlic; stir to brown garlic. Add mushrooms and
lettuce. Stir and toss until vegetables are wilted
and just heated through. Season with sugar, sherry,
soy sauce and more salt, if needed. Toss well and
serve immediately.

STIR-FRIED SNOW PEAS WITH PRAWNS
3 or 4 servings

1/2 lb. snow peas, see below

 1 8-oz. can straw mushrooms, drained and halved

10 fresh water chestnuts, peeled and sliced
    (canned water chestnuts may be substituted)

 1 slice peeled fresh ginger

 1 to 2 teaspoons cream sherry

oil   chicken broth   ground pepper

salt to taste, about 1/8 teaspoon

1/2 lb. medium prawns, shelled, deveined, halved
     lengthwise and marinated in:

    1/4 teaspoon salt

    pinch ground pepper

    1/2 teaspoon sesame oil

    1 teaspoon thin soy sauce

Mix:

    1 tablespoon cornstarch

    1/2 tablespoon soy sauce

    3/4 cup chicken broth

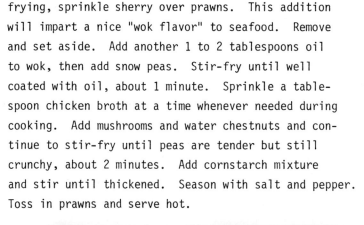

Pinch off both ends of snow peas, remove strings
(if any), wash and drain.

Heat wok over high heat; add 1 tablespoon oil.
When oil is hot, add ginger; brown. Add prawns;
stir-fry until cooked, 2 to 3 minutes. While stir-

frying, sprinkle sherry over prawns. This addition
will impart a nice "wok flavor" to seafood. Remove
and set aside. Add another 1 to 2 tablespoons oil
to wok, then add snow peas. Stir-fry until well
coated with oil, about 1 minute. Sprinkle a tablespoon chicken broth at a time whenever needed during
cooking. Add mushrooms and water chestnuts and continue to stir-fry until peas are tender but still
crunchy, about 2 minutes. Add cornstarch mixture
and stir until thickened. Season with salt and pepper.
Toss in prawns and serve hot.

STIR FRIED BROCCOLI WITH BEEF
4 servings

2   slices peeled ginger

1   bunch broccoli, cut as instructed below

oil for cooking

salt and pepper to taste

3/4   lb. flank steak (top sirloin or chuck),
      thinly sliced against grain, marinated in:

    1/2   teaspoon beef bouillon powder (optional)

    1/2   teaspoon salt

    1/8   teaspoon ground pepper

      1   tablespoon cornstarch

    1/2   teaspoon sesame oil

    1/2   tablespoon *each* sherry and soy sauce

Mix:

    1-1/4   teaspoons cornstarch

    1/2   cup beef broth

Peel off the outer covering of the lower parts along the main stems of broccoli. Diagonally slice main stems into 3/16" thickness. Cut remaining smaller parts into 1" flowerettes.

Heat wok over high heat until hot; add 2 tablespoons oil. When hot, add ginger; brown to extract flavor. Add beef and stir-fry to desired doneness, about 1-1/2 minutes. Remove beef and set aside.

Again, heat wok. Add 1 to 2 tablespoons oil. When hot, add broccoli. Stir and toss for about 3 minutes or until crisp-tender, sprinkling 1 to 2 tablespoons water at a time when wok appears dry and as needed. The addition of liquid to the dry hot wok will create steam and sizzle, imparting a nice wok flavor to food. (Thinly sliced broccoli and other high water content vegetables can be stir-fried by this method very nicely.) Stir in gravy mixture; toss until thickened. Add a little more broth if a thinner gravy is desired. Add meat and season with salt and pepper. Serve.

VEGETARIAN FOOD
5 or 6 servings

  2 tablespoons oil

  2 slices peeled fresh ginger

1/2 teaspoon salt

  1 tablespoon wet bean curd, see wet bean curd in INGREDIENTS

  5 or 6 dried Chinese mushrooms, soaked to soften, stems removed, sliced

  2 to 3 tablespoons dried cloud ears, soaked to soften, hard stems removed (cut big "ears" in halves)

  4 oz. bamboo shoots or water chestnuts, sliced

3/4 cup water

  1 cup chicken broth

 20 golden needles (lily buds), soaked to soften, stems removed, halved

  2 oz. bean threads (vermicelli), deep-fried, broken into 4"-5" lengths

1/2 to 3/4 lb. green vegetable, such as snow peas, bok choy, yard-long beans, Chinese okra (see below*)

1/2 lb. bean sprouts

soy sauce or salt to taste, if needed

Heat wok until hot. Add oil. When oil is hot, add ginger and brown to extract flavor; then add salt and wet bean curd. After stirring a few times, add mushrooms, cloud ears and bamboo shoots. Stir-fry until well coated with oil and sauce, then add water and broth. Cover and steam for 2 minutes. Add golden needles and fried bean threads; cover and cook one minute. Add green vegetable; stir and mix. Cook as directed below. Add bean sprouts during the last 1-1/2 minutes of cooking, stirring and tossing constantly. Season with soy sauce and/or salt. Serve.

* 1/4 to 1/3 lb. snow peas, diagonally cut in 3 or 4 pieces, cover and cook 2 to 3 minutes

  1/2 lb. bok choy, cut in 1-1/2" bite-sized pieces, cover and cook about 3 minutes

  1/3 lb. Chinese yard-long beans, cut in 1-1/2" lengths, cover and cook 2-1/2 to 3 minutes

  2 or 3 Chinese okra, peeled and sliced, add with bean sprouts during the last 1-1/2 minutes of cooking

VEGETARIAN VEGETABLE STIR FRY
4 servings

oil for cooking

- 1 slice peeled ginger, crushed
- 1 medium-sized carrot, pared, sliced, parboiled until crisp-tender
- 1/2 can tender baby corn, cut long ears in halves
- 1/2 cup sliced bamboo shoots
- 2 4"x1-1/2" sized deep-fried bean curd (available in produce section), cut in small strips
- 10 cloud ears, soaked, well-rinsed, stems removed, squeezed dry (cut large "ears" into 2 or 3 smaller pieces)
- 1/2 cup chicken broth, more if needed
- 1/4 lb. fresh mushrooms, sliced
- 1 green onion (or equal amount of Chinese chives) cut in 1-1/2" lengths

salt or soy sauce to taste

ground pepper

Set wok over high heat until very hot. Add 1-1/2 tablespoons oil and 1/4 teaspoon salt, then add ginger; brown to extract flavor. Add carrot, baby corn, bamboo shoots, fried bean curd, and cloud ears; stir and toss until well coated with the seasoning. Add broth, cover and cook for about 2 minutes. (If there is too much liquid, cook a little longer, uncovered. There is no gravy in this dish, but the food should not be burned or dry.) Uncover wok, add mushrooms. Toss and mix until mushrooms are heated through, then add green onion. Turn heat off. Season with pepper and salt or soy sauce. The dish, at this point, should just be moist and almost waterless.

BEEF AND ASPARAGUS
3 or 4 servings

1   bunch asparagus, cleaned, diagonally cut tender
    parts into 1/4" thick slices
2   cloves garlic, crushed
1   slice peeled ginger
oil   beef broth   soy sauce   salt
ground pepper or onion powder
3/4 lb. flank steak (top sirloin or chuck), thinly
     sliced against grain and marinated in:

    1-1/2 tablespoons cornstarch

       1 teaspoon *each* sesame oil and oil

      1/2 teaspoon salt

      1/8 teaspoon ground pepper

      1/2 tablespoon *each* cream sherry (or any
          kind of sherry or Chinese rice wine)
          and soy sauce

Gravy: mix

    1-1/4 teaspoons cornstarch
     1/2 cup beef broth

Set wok over high heat. Add 2 tablespoons oil.
When oil is hot, add garlic and ginger and brown
to extract flavor. Add meat and stir-fry to desired doneness, 1 to 2 minutes. Remove from wok
and set aside.

Add another tablespoon oil to wok, then add a pinch
of salt and asparagus. Stir and toss until tender
but still crunchy and emerald green, sprinkling
broth, a tablespoon at a time, over asparagus as
needed during stir-frying. Add gravy, bring to a
fast boil. Total cooking time for asparagus is
approximately 3 minutes. Remove from heat. Season
with soy sauce, salt and pepper or onion powder to
taste. Spoon into server. Top with beef.

PORK AND LOTUS ROOT STIR FRY
3 servings

oil for cooking

1 thin slice ginger

8 to 10 oz. (1 medium-sized section) fresh lotus root, scrubbed and rinsed, peeled, rinsed again, thinly sliced lengthwise into 2"x1"x1/6" thick pieces

2 or 3 fresh water chestnuts, peeled, rinsed, thinly sliced

4 to 6 fresh mushrooms, cleaned, sliced

3/4 cup chicken broth (or half water half broth, if broth is salty), more if needed

1 green onion, cut in 1" lengths

1/2 teaspoon sugar

salt or thin soy sauce to taste

1/4 lb. (net weight) shredded lean pork, marinated in:

    1 teaspoon cornstarch

    1/4 teaspoon salt

    a pinch of ground white pepper

    1/2 teaspoon thin soy sauce

Heat wok over high heat until hot. Add 2 to 3 teaspoons oil and ginger; stir to brown ginger. Add pork; stir-fry until cooked through, about 3 minutes. Remove and set aside.

Reheat wok. Add 1 tablespoon oil and a pinch of salt. Swirl around, then add lotus root. Quickly stir and toss until well mixed with salt and oil, then add broth. Cover and steam-cook for 2-1/2 to 3 minutes. Uncover, add water chestnuts and mushrooms; stir and toss until all vegetables are cooked through, another minute or two. Add more broth or water if wok is dry. The starch from lotus root makes a satiny glaze. (No need to add gravy.) Finally add green onion, sugar, and pork; mix well. Season with salt or thin soy sauce, if needed.

Stir-fried lotus root is crunchy, refreshing and delicious.

CHINESE RADISHES WITH BEEF
2 servings

oil for cooking

2 slices ginger, crushed

1 lb. Chinese white radishes (also called Chinese turnips) or Japanese daikon, peeled, cut in 1/4" thick bite-sized slices

1/8 teaspoon sugar

1/3 to 1/2 cup beef broth or water

1/2 to 1 green onion, cut in 1" lengths

salt and ground pepper

1/2 lb. (net weight) all lean top sirloin, chuck or flank steak, shredded across the grain into matchstick size, marinated in:

    1 tablespoon cornstarch

    1/4 plus 1/8 teaspoon salt

    pinch ground pepper

    1/2 teaspoon *each* sherry, sesame oil and thin soy sauce

Heat wok until very hot. Add 1 tablespoon oil and 1 slice ginger; brown to extract flavor. Add beef; stir-fry to desired doneness, about 1-1/2 minutes. Remove and set aside.

Reheat wok. Add 2 to 3 teaspoons oil, 1/8 teaspoon salt and 1 slice ginger; brown to extract ginger flavor. Add radishes; stir until well coated with seasoning. Add sugar and liquid. Cover and cook over medium-high heat until tender, about 10 minutes. If there is too much liquid, uncover and cook over high heat during the last 3 or 4 minutes of cooking. There should be little or almost no liquid. Add onion; mix. Season with more salt and/or ground pepper to taste. Spoon into server. Top with beef.

STIR-FRIED BEANS
4 or 5 servings

1/2 recipe BASIC STIR-FRIED PORK, page 43

1 lb. Chinese yard-long beans or Kentucky wonder beans, cut in 1-1/2" lengths

3/4 cup water (or half water, half chicken broth), more liquid if needed during cooking

1 teaspoon soy sauce

salt and ground pepper to taste

oil for cooking

Gravy: mix

    1-1/2 teaspoons cornstarch

    1/4 cup chicken broth or water

Stir-fry pork as directed; omit the addition of green onion. Set aside.

Heat wok over high heat. When hot, add 1 to 1-1/2 tablespoons oil and 1/4 teaspoon salt. When hot, add beans. Stir to coat with oil for 1 minute. Add water; cover and steam over medium-high to high heat until crisp-tender (2 to 3 minutes for yard-long beans, 3 to 5 minutes for green beans, depending on freshness and quality). Add gravy and pork; stir until thickened. Turn heat off. Season with soy sauce, pepper and more salt if needed.

CUCUMBERS WITH SHRIMP
3 or 4 servings

1 tablespoon oil

1/8 teaspoon salt, more or less to taste

1 slice ginger

2 heaping tablespoons dried shrimp, soaked for 10 minutes, picked over or deveined, rinsed, soaked again 20 minutes, drained and liquid reserved for cooking

2 garden-fresh cucumbers (1 to 1-1/4 lb.) peeled lengthwise at 3/4" intervals, cut in half lengthwise, then cut halves crosswise into 1/4" slices

1/4 cup liquid, containing "shrimp water" above

5 or 6 fresh mushrooms, sliced

a sprinkle *each* of ground white pepper and sesame oil

Set wok over high heat until hot. Add oil, salt and ginger; stir around several times to extract ginger flavor. Add shrimp, stir-fry 1/2 to 1 minute. Add cucumbers; toss and stir for 1/2 minute or until well mixed with other ingredients in wok. Pour in liquid and continue to stir and toss 1-1/2 minutes. Toss in mushrooms. Stir-fry for 2 more minutes. There should be little or no liquid. Season with ground pepper and sesame oil.

FIVE-FLAVORED CABBAGE STIR FRY
4 servings

1 small head (1 to 1-1/4 lb.) green cabbage, cut into bite-sized pieces

2 small carrots, peeled, cut into 1/8" thick slices, parboiled for 2 to 3 minutes until crisp-tender

6 to 8 peeled water chestnuts (preferably fresh ones), each cut into 3 or 4 slices

15 canned whole button mushrooms (or 6 fresh mushrooms, sliced)

1/2 to 1 cup sliced char shiu (CANTONESE ROASTED PORK, see recipe), may be omitted for vegetarian dish

1/2 teaspoon sugar (optional)   chicken broth

salt (about 1/4 teaspoon)

ground pepper (optional)   oil for cooking

Heat wok until hot. Add 1 to 2 tablespoons oil and 1/4 teaspoon salt; swirl a few times. Add vegetables; toss as quickly as you can. Sprinkle 1 to 2 tablespoons broth over vegetables when wok appears dry and as needed. Continue to stir and toss until cabbage is limp and just cooked through, 4 to 5 minutes. Add meat and sugar; mix. Remove wok from heat. Season with pepper and more salt, if needed. This dish appears to be "dry" and waterless. The cabbage should still be crunchy. Green cabbage stir-fried by this technique is simply delicious.

CHICKEN CORN SOUP
4-6 servings

1 can (13-3/4 oz.) chicken broth

2 cups water

2 heaping cups frozen or canned corn kernels, chopped

1 egg, beaten

1 green onion, very finely cut

ground white pepper   salt (about 1/8 teaspoon)

1 small chicken breast, skinned, boned, diced the size of corn kernel, and mixed with:

   1/8 teaspoon salt

   2 teaspoons *each* cornstarch, thin soy sauce and cooking oil

Mix:

   3 tablespoons cornstarch

   1 teaspoon sesame oil

   2 tablespoons water

   2 teaspoons cream sherry

Bring broth and water to a boil. Add corn; stir and bring to a boil. Stir in cornstarch mixture until clear. Spoon out 1/4 cup of soup; add it to chicken and mix well. Now, add chicken to soup and stir until meat turns white, 1/2 to 1 minute. Turn heat off. Pour egg in a thin stream, while stirring in a circular motion to form "egg flower" shreds. Finally add onion and season soup with pepper and salt to taste.

REFRESHING VEGETABLE SOUP
3 or 4 servings

2   small carrots, peeled, cut into thin slices 1/8" to 1/4" thick
5   or 6 peeled fresh (preferably) or canned water chestnuts, each cut into 5 or 6 slices
3/4 lb. (approximately) napa cabbage or celery cabbage, cut into bite-sized pieces
1-1/2 cups water
1-1/2 cups clear chicken (or beef) broth
salt, if needed

In a medium-sized saucepan, bring water and broth to a boil. Add carrots, reduce heat, cover pan, and cook until carrots are crisp-tender, about 5 minutes. Add water chestnuts and cabbage. Stir and bring to a full boil over high heat. Stir again and salt to taste.

STIR-FRIED SPINACH
2 servings

1   bunch (about 1 lb.) fresh spinach, washed, cut in 3" lengths
1   tablespoon oil
1   small clove garlic, crushed
1/4 teaspoon sesame oil
1/8 teaspoon sugar
salt to taste

Drop spinach into rapidly boiling water for 1/2 to 1 minute, turning spinach over once or twice. Drain. Rinse with cold water. Drain again.

Heat wok until hot. Add oil. When oil is hot, add garlic and brown to extract flavor. Add spinach and stir-fry until hot and well mixed with oil. Add sesame oil, sugar and salt to taste.

BEAN THREADS WITH STIR-FRIED MEAT
3 or 4 servings

2 oz. mung bean threads, soaked for at least 30 minutes or until soft, cut in manageable lengths, drained

1 cup chicken broth or homemade stock

1 cup water, more if needed

1 to 2 cups green vegetables, cut in bite-sized pieces (such as 2 cups bok choy, 1 cup sliced asparagus, beans or snow peas)

1 cup stir-fried meat or seafood of your choice, see beef, pork, chicken or seafood recipes

soy sauce, salt, ground pepper and sesame oil to taste

Stir-fry meat or seafood according to recipe. (Leftover meat can be substituted.)

Add chicken broth and water to bean threads. Bring to a boil, then reduce heat and slow simmer for 10 minutes. Add vegetables; stir and cook over higher heat for 3 to 4 minutes or until vegetables are cooked through. Mix in meat and season with soy sauce, salt, pepper and sesame oil. There should be little or no liquid. Serve as a vegetable dish.

LOTUS ROOT SOUP
4 servings

1 lb. fresh lotus root, scraped (get dirt off!) and rinsed, peeled, washed, cut across into 1" sections (or leave whole and cut after cooking)

3 dried salted duck gizzards, rinsed (or 1/4 lb. all lean pork, parboiled for a few minutes to get rid of foam)

5 dried Chinese red dates, soaked

1 3/4" square dried Chinese tangerine peel, soaked

5 or 6 water chestnuts (canned or fresh), sliced

3 dried Chinese mushrooms, soaked, destemmed

4-1/2 cups water (add another 1/2 cup if needed)

salt

Place lotus root, gizzards or pork, dates, tangerine peel, water chestnuts, mushrooms and water in a 4-quart saucepan. Bring to a boil. Reduce heat to medium-low and simmer until lotus root is tender, 1-1/4 to 1-1/2 hours. Pick out and discard dates and tangerine peel. Also remove gizzards, and cut into slices. Add gizzard slices back to soup or serve separately for snacks. Salt soup to taste. Serve. Lotus root is expensive but refreshingly sweet. See photo on page 198.

SEAWEED TOFU SOUP
5 or 6 servings

3/4 to 1 oz. dried seaweed*

3 cups water

1 small carrot, peeled and thinly sliced

5 fresh water chestnuts, peeled and sliced

1 21-oz. carton fresh medium-firm or firm tofu, cut into bite-sized cubes

1 13-3/4 oz. can chicken broth (or pork bones)

salt to taste (start with 1/8 teaspoon)

Soak seaweed in a large pan of water for at least 30 minutes. Seaweed is now soft and expanded. A "whole" seaweed is somewhat mushroom-shaped. Remove "stems" and all hard and foreign matter such as sand, weeds and shell pieces. Wash several times until clean. Drain. Cut large pieces smaller. You should have about 1 cup.

Bring water and seaweed to a boil, then simmer over low heat for 50 minutes. Add carrot and chicken broth; bring to a fast boil over high heat and cook until carrot slices are crisp-tender, 2 to 3 minutes. Add water chestnuts and bean curd. When it comes to a boil again, turn off heat. Salt to taste.

If you use pork bones, omit chicken broth. Parboil bones and rinse with cold water until all foaming substances are gone. Add bones and two more cups of water at the start. After soup has simmered for 50 minutes, remove bones, skim out fat, then proceed as directed above.

Seaweed soup is commonly served in the summer, although it may seem strange to serve hot soup in the summer heat. It is soothing and refreshing.

* This is the regular dried purple seaweed, not the well-processed, pressed, instant and ready-to-use type.

WINTER MELON POND
6-8 servings

1   small whole winter melon (at least 5-6 lb)

3   to 6 dried Chinese red dates, soaked for 10 minutes

3   to 6 dried Chinese mushrooms, soaked until soft, stems removed, cut in slices

2   dried salted duck gizzards, rinsed and soaked for 10 minutes (save this water for filling melon)

1/4 to 1/3 cup sliced water chestnuts or bamboo shoots

1   small piece dried Chinese tangerine peel

mixture of 3 parts chicken broth and 1 part water, boiling hot

1   teaspoon finely cut green onion

salt and pepper to taste

1/2 cup thinly sliced skinless and boneless chicken (pork, shrimp or any combination), marinated in:

    1/4 teaspoon salt

    1   tablespoon cornstarch

    1   tablespoon thin soy sauce

    2   tablespoons chicken broth (add this to meat and mix well just before adding meat to soup)

Cut off top of melon with the stem end (cut in zig-zag pattern for a fancier appearance); save it for lid. Scoop out pulp and seeds; discard. Scrape exterior. Rinse inside and outside until clean; drain.

Place dates, mushrooms, gizzards, water chestnuts and tangerine peel inside melon. Add chicken broth-water mixture to fill melon 3/4 full. Cover melon with its own lid. Set melon in a steaming bowl, then place bowl on a rack in a large pot filled with water. Replenish with boiling water as needed. Steam until melon flesh is tender, 1 to 2 hours for a small melon or 2 to 4 hours for a large mature melon. Add meat to soup and steam until soup content is cooked through and the meat is just tenderly done. Pick out gizzards, slice, then return to soup. Add green onion, salt and pepper. Serve soup with pieces of melon flesh.

If desired, carve a design or Chinese character on melon. Winter melon pond is an attractive gourmet specialty, sometimes filled with bird's nest soup or shark fin soup.

MELON AND CORN SOUP
4 to 6 servings

2 cups water for soup, more if needed during cooking

2 lb. winter melon, seeds and pulp removed, peeled, diced in 1/2" chunks (about 5 cups)

1-1/2 cups clear chicken broth for soup

2 cups tender corn kernels, canned or frozen

5 fresh mushrooms, chopped

1 10-3/4 oz. can cream of mushroom soup

1 green onion, minced or chopped

salt and pepper to taste

1/2 chicken breast, skinned, boned, coarsely minced (or 1/2 cup minced lean pork or diced shrimp), marinated in:

    1/4 teaspoon salt

    1 teaspoon cornstarch

    1 teaspoon thin soy sauce

    1 teaspoon sesame oil

Thickener: mix

    2 tablespoons cornstarch

    2 tablespoons water

Bring water to a boil. Add winter melon. Bring it back to a boil. Reduce heat to medium-low and cook for 45 to 60 minutes or until the winter melon is very soft and slightly mushy. Add chicken broth, corn, fresh mushrooms and mushroom soup; bring to a boil and cook for about 2 minutes. (If you are not ready to serve the soup at this point, turn heat off. When ready, bring it back to a boil, then proceed as directed below.) Add thickener; stir until cooked through. Spoon a big scoop of soup into chicken meat, stir to mix, then add chicken and green onion to soup. Stir until meat is tenderly cooked, 1 minute or less. Remove from heat. Season with salt and pepper to taste. This soup makes a satisfying low-cal one-pot meal.

CHICKEN SALAD WITH GARLIC-SOY DRESSING
6 to 8 servings

1/2 large head iceberg lettuce (rinse, pat dry, shred)

2 small carrots, peeled, thinly shredded

1 cucumber, peeled, shredded

2 to 3 cups shredded roasted chicken meat, see below

2 oz. (or 1/4 to 1/2 cup) barbecue-flavored (or smoked) almonds, crushed

2 oz. rice sticks, deep-fried (see below), lightly crumbled into shorter lengths

Garlic-Soy Dressing:

    3 or 4 cloves garlic, finely minced

    1 to 1-1/2 tablespoons salad oil

    1/2 teaspoon Chinese 5-spice

    1/4 teaspoon ground white pepper

    1/2 cup drippings from roasted chicken

    1/4 cup thin soy sauce

    1/2 tablespoon sesame oil

    salt, if needed to make dressing taste a little salty

Roast a large chicken, using your favorite recipe. Skim and discard fat from drippings. Reserve drippings for dressing. This part can be done one or two days in advance. Reheat drippings if chilled.

Loosen rice sticks. Taking a small handful at a time, lower into 365° F. oil and immediately turn over to fry until puffy and expanded. This takes only a few seconds. Be sure every strand is fried and puffy. If fried in advance, store at room temperature. Reheat in slow oven to restore crispness.

Heat a heavy-bottomed small saucepan until hot. Add oil and garlic; stir until garlic is golden, but not brown. Remove saucepan from heat. Add remaining dressing ingredients. Stir until well mixed. Cool.

In a large salad bowl, toss lettuce, carrots, cucumber, and chicken together with some (much or little, to taste) dressing. Sprinkle almonds over salad, then top with most of fried rice sticks. Serve immediately. Set remaining dressing and rice sticks on table for extra helpings.

GOLD MOUNTAIN PINEAPPLE CHICKEN SALAD
4 servings

1 oz. bean threads (vermicelli), soaked for 30 minutes, cut into 4-5" lengths, boiled in water for 5 minutes, drained, rinsed with cold water, drained again*

1 small carrot, peeled, shredded into toothpick size

1/2 roasted or deep-fried chicken breast, skinned, deboned, and shredded by hand

2 cucumbers (not too large), shredded

1 8-1/4 oz. can crushed pineapple in heavy syrup, drained; reserve syrup for dressing

1 tablespoon roasted white sesame seeds

Rich Peanut Butter Dressing: Mix the dry ingredients thoroughly, then gradually add remaining ingredients and blend well. Makes 3/4 cup.

1/8 teaspoon Chinese chili powder

1/4 scant teaspoon Chinese 5-spice

1/8 to 1/4 teaspoon salt, depending on personal taste

2 tablespoons *each* brown sugar and dark soy sauce

1/2 tablespoon sesame oil

1/4 cup smooth peanut butter

1 tablespoon oil

4 tablespoons white vinegar

2 tablespoons reserved pineapple syrup, see above

Creamy Curry Dressing: Mix the dry ingredients first, then gradually add remaining ingredients and blend well. Makes 3/4 cup.

1/2 teaspoon *each* dry mustard and curry powder

1 tablespoon sugar

1/8 teaspoon *each* ground pepper and salt

6 tablespoons real mayonnaise

1/2 tablespoon sesame oil

2-1/2 tablespoons white vinegar

2 tablespoons reserved pineapple syrup

Select a large round platter. Line well-drained cold vermicelli on platter as the first layer. The second layer is cucumber; make the concentric circle slightly smaller so the vermicelli will show outside the circumference of cucumber circle. The third layer is chicken, a smaller circle than the second layer so the cucumber will show around the edges. The fourth layer is pineapple, smaller than the chicken layer. The fifth and final layer is carrot, the smallest circle of all. You now have built a frustum (a figure formed by cutting off the top of a cone). Sprinkle sesame seeds over "gold mountain". Refrigerate until ready to serve. You may serve it with peanut butter dress-

GOLD MOUNTAIN PINEAPPLE CHICKEN SALAD
(continued)

ing or curry dressing on the side and let each diner help himself or herself. Or, after the "show", pour dressing over salad, toss and serve.

* For variation, deep-fry *dry* bean threads, see rice sticks used in CHICKEN SALAD WITH GARLIC-SOY DRESSING for reference. Crush fried bean threads and sprinkle *over* the top (other four layers remain in same order) to create a "snowy mountain".

CAULIFLOWER IN HAM SAUCE
3 or 4 servings

1	head (about 1-1/4 lb.) cauliflower, cut in bite-sized flowerettes
3/4	cup water
1/2	cup finely minced cooked ham (turkey ham or Chinese ham)

oil for cooking   salt

Thickener: mix

2	teaspoons cornstarch
1/4	cup clear chicken broth
1	slice peeled ginger, well minced (this dish is mildly flavored with ginger; the spicier version may use 3 or 4 slices of ginger)
1	teaspoon thin soy sauce

Heat wok until very hot. Add 1-1/2 to 2 tablespoons oil and 1/8 teaspoon salt; stir a few times. Add cauliflower and stir-fry for 1 minute until well coated with oil-salt mixture. Add water; cover and cook over high heat for 3 minutes. Uncover; stir. Add thickener; stir until clear. Add ham; mix. Serve.

GINGER SALAD
6 to 8 servings

1/2   lb. mung bean sprouts (pick over, parboil for 10 seconds, drain, plunge into cold water, then drain again)

2   small carrots, peeled, then shaved into shreds with potato peeler

1   bunch fresh spinach (thoroughly rinse, pick over, cut stems in 1-1/2" lengths and leaves in coarse shreds)

2   oranges, peeled, sectioned, then cut into small chunks (pineapple chunks may be substituted)

Dressing:

2   tablespoons oil

1   tablespoon finely minced fresh ginger (more ginger if desired)

salt and ground pepper to taste, if needed

mix together:

1   teaspoon sesame oil

3   tablespoons *each* brown sugar, thin soy sauce and white vinegar

1/2   cup chicken broth

Heat a heavy-bottomed saucepan until very hot. Add oil; swirl. Add ginger and stir; do not brown ginger. Pour in liquid mixture and bring to a boil. Season with salt and pepper to taste. Cool. Just before serving, toss well-drained vegetables and oranges in a salad bowl. Serve with dressing.

FAMILY-STYLE BEAN CURD
4 servings

1/2   to 1 cup stir-fried meat (see recipes) or left-over meat (chicken, pork or beef), optional

16   oz. medium-firm fresh tofu, drained, cut into 1-1/2" cubes

1/4   cup *each* chicken broth and water, more water if needed

1   teaspoon soy sauce (or 2 teaspoons oyster sauce)

1/8   teaspoon salt or to taste

1   green onion, chopped

pinch ground white pepper

Sauce: mix

1   tablespoon cornstarch

1/4   cup chicken broth

Have leftover meat ready or stir-fry meat according to directions.

Heat wok. Add as little oil as possible and only if needed; swirl a few times. Add tofu, chicken broth and water. Bring to a fast boil and allow contents to only cook through. Pour in sauce; gently turn and stir until bubbly and thickened. Season with soy sauce, pepper, salt, and add green onion and meat. Gently mix. Serve with rice. For variations, add curry powder or chili powder to taste.

makes 6 to 7 cups

4 links (2 pairs) Chinese pork sausage, diced

4 medium-sized carrots, peeled, diced

about 1 cup water, more or less

4 stalks celery, diced

1/2 to 3/4 cup ready-to-eat cooked chestnut meats, chopped

7 or 8 oz. herb seasoned croutons or stuffing mix

1/2 cup drippings (skim fat) from roasted turkey or roasted chicken

about 1 cup chicken broth, more or less

2 green onions, chopped

salt and ground pepper to taste

Pan-fry sausage over low heat until golden brown, stirring often. Drain oil. Set meat aside.

Set wok or a heavy-bottomed large Dutch oven over high heat until hot. Add 2 tablespoons oil and 1/8 teaspoon salt. Stir a few times. Add carrots; stir until well mixed with oil. Add about 1/2 cup water to barely cover the carrots. Cover with lid and steam over medium heat until crisp-tender, 3 to 4 minutes. Uncover, add celery, mix, and add another 1/2 cup (more or less) water to just cover the vegetables. Cover with lid and steam until vegetables are very tender but still retain their shapes. Add sausage, chestnuts, croutons, drippings and enough chicken broth to make a moist stuffing. Mix well. Season with pepper and salt to taste. Set over simmering heat for 10 to 15 minutes. Stir from time to time and add more chicken broth or water, if needed. Finally add green onions; mix. Serve as is or use it to stuff chicken, duck or a small turkey.

BEAN-CURD PUFFS
makes 9 stuffed puffs

1 package deep-fried bean-curd cake (3 4"x1-1/2" logs)

1 to 2 tablespoons oil for pan-frying

Filling: mix together

    1/2 lb. lean pork, minced

    6 canned or fresh water chestnuts, minced

    1 slice peeled ginger, finely minced

    2 tablespoons minced green onion

    dash ground pepper

    1/4 teaspoon salt

    1 tablespoon *each* cornstarch and fish sauce (or thin soy sauce)

Blend:

    1 teaspoon cornstarch

    1/4 cup chicken broth, more if needed during cooking

Cut bean curd logs, crosswise, into thirds. Gently pull and open the center of each puff to form a cup. Stuff with filling. Heat oil and fry puffs with meat side down until golden brown. Spoon out any excess oil. Turn the pieces over. Add cornstarch mixture, cover and slow simmer for 4 to 5 minutes. Add a little more chicken broth or water if sauce is too thick. Serve for dim sum or as a side dish for dinner.

BRAISED MUSHROOMS
12 stuffed mushrooms

12 large dried Chinese mushrooms, soaked to soften, destemmed

2 to 3 tablespoons oil for pan-frying

all-purpose flour for dusting

Filling: mix together

    1/4 lb. prawns, shelled, deveined, minced

    1/4 lb. lean pork, minced

    1/2 tablespoon *each* cornstarch and fish sauce (thin soy sauce may be used)

    1/8 teaspoon ground ginger or grated fresh ginger

    1/4 teaspoon salt

    1 tablespoon minced green onion

    3 to 4 tablespoons minced bamboo shoots

Blend:

    1 teaspoon *each* cornstarch and sesame oil

    1/4 cup clear chicken broth

Cook mushrooms in as little water as possible until tender. Squeeze out excess liquid. Dust caps (stem side only) with flour, then stuff with filling. Pan-fry mushrooms, meat side down, in hot oil until golden, 2 to 3 minutes. Spoon out excess oil. Turn mushrooms over. Add 2 to 4 tablespoons water, cover and simmer for 3 to 4 minutes. Add cornstarch mixture; cook until thickened. Serve hot.

RICE & NOODLES

PLAIN LONG-GRAIN RICE
about 6 cups

2 cups long-grain rice, rinsed 4 or 5 times or until water is clear, drained

3 cups minus 3 tablespoons water for firmer texture or 3 cups water for softer texture*

Pour water and rice into a heavy-bottomed medium saucepan (a saucepan with a heavy tight-fitting lid is best). Set aside for 15 to 30 minutes. Bring to a boil over high heat, then give contents a thorough stir. Reduce heat to medium-high and continue to boil until the water is absorbed and small "craters" appear on the surface, 5 to 6 minutes after rice starts to boil. From now on, keep the lid on tightly and do not peek. Decrease to low heat and let rice simmer for 5 minutes. Turn heat to simmer and slowly cook for another 12 minutes. Rice is now done. Uncover and fluff the grains with chopsticks. Turn heat off. Keep rice covered until ready to serve.

To reheat, steam rice in a bowl above boiling water until soft and hot.

To measure the water the Chinese way: Add water, without measuring, to rinsed rice. Evenly level rice. Vertically hold a middle finger on top of rice. When water is at the same level as the first knuckle (first joint), it is the right amount of water. This method works every time and it eliminates the time and effort of measuring. Eventually, most cooks can measure the amount of water by sight. Experience has shown that water evaporates at a faster rate when rice is cooking over a gas stove. Add 2 to 3 tablespoons more water to rice at the start or sprinkle 2 to 3 tablespoons water over rice during cooking.

* Rice cooking is a very personal affair. Some like it firm and some like it soft. The gourmet connoisseur may describe firmer steamed rice as having "a good aromatic flavor" and soft steamed rice as "bland and tasteless".

PLAIN SHORT-GRAIN RICE
about 6 cups

2 cups Cal Rose rice (or other short-grain rice*), rinsed 4 or 5 times or until water is clear, drained

2-1/3 cups water for firmer texture or 2-1/2 cups water for softer texture

Pour water and rice into a heavy-bottomed medium saucepan. Set aside for 15 to 30 minutes. Bring to a boil over high heat, then give contents a thorough stir. Reduce heat to medium-high and continue to boil until the water is absorbed and small "craters" appear on the surface, about four minutes after rice starts to boil. From this point on, keep the lid on tightly and do not peek. Decrease to low heat and let rice simmer for four minutes. Turn heat down to simmer; let rice slowly cook for another 15 minutes. Uncover and fluff up the grains. Turn heat off. Keep covered until serving.

To reheat, steam rice in a bowl above boiling water until soft and hot. See PLAIN LONG-GRAIN RICE for reference.

* To cook glutinous rice, see FRIED SWEET RICE, page 141.

SWEET TAMALES
7 or 8 rice tamales

3 cups glutinous rice (sweet rice)

1/2 cup Chinese red beans (dried red beans)

salt

bamboo leaves

one ball 12 lb. strength white parcel post twine

Serving Accompaniment:

honey, syrup or mix 1/4 cup sugar with 1/2 teaspoon cinnamon

Soak leaves overnight. Wash thoroughly. Discard torn leaves. Scald in boiling water for 5 minutes. Drain. Separately, wash, then soak rice and beans overnight. Drain. Add 3/4 teaspoon salt to rice; mix. Add pinch of salt to beans; mix. Make and cook these sweet tamales as directed in CHINESE RICE TAMALES, omitting salt in boiling water. For each tamale, use approximately 12 tablespoons rice with 3 tablespoons bean in the center. Serve warm or cold with syrup, honey or cinnamon-sugar.

See photo on page 16, and wrapping directions on pages 138 and 139.

CHINESE RICE TAMALES
makes 7 or 8 tamales

3   cups sweet rice (glutinous rice)
1   cup yellow split peas
4   links Chinese pork sausage
3   salted duck egg yolks, each cut in 6 strips
1   ball 12-lb. strength white parcel post twine
bamboo leaves
salt

Soak leaves overnight. Wash thoroughly. Discard
torn leaves. Scald in boiling water for 5 minutes.
Drain, but do not dry.

Separately, wash, then soak rice and peas overnight. Drain.

Scrape preserving materials off salted duck eggs.
Wash well. Shell eggs and cut yolks. Discard
whites or reserve for other uses. (Beaten whites
can be added to jook, for example. See FISH JOOK.)

Rinse sausages and pat dry. Cut in halves.

Add 1-1/4 teaspoons salt to rice; mix. Add 1/4
teaspoon salt to peas; mix.

Select a large bamboo leaf. Fold it crosswise in
half. Fold again lengthwise in half. Lift one layer of leaf, leaving other 3 layers together. Result
will look like a lunch bag cut lengthwise in half.
Holding the leaf bag in one hand, line the interior
with 6 tablespoons rice, spreading to approximately
4" in length along the bag. Line the rice with 3
tablespoons peas, leaving about 3/8" unlined rice
edge all the way around. Place a piece of sausage
and 2 or 3 strips of yolk in the center of the peas.
Cover sausage and yolk with another 3 tablespoons
of peas, then cover peas with 6 more tablespoons of
rice to complete the filling. As the bag is being
filled, add leaves around the edge of the bag, always place leaves overlapping each other. When
filling is completed, bring side leaves together
and fold over toward the center. Next, fold the
open end toward the center. Tie with twine crosswise from one end to the other, then tie lengthwise 2 or 3 times. The tamale is done and has di-
mensions of 3"x5"x2". If tamales are tied too
tightly, the rice will be hard to the taste. On
the other hand, if tamales are tied too loosely,
the rice will burst out during cooking. Each tamale

takes about 4 good leaves, but use as many as needed to reinforce cracks. Dry leftover leaves indoors for other or future uses.

Place tamales on low cake rack (so water can circulate underneath) in a large pot having a tight lid. Cover with water at least 2" above the top of tamales, replenishing with boiling water every 30 to 45 minutes. Add 1-1/2 tablespoons salt to water. Cover and bring to a full boil. Reduce heat and boil for 4-1/2 to 5 hours. After cooking, remove tamales to racks to cool. Unwrap and cut in fourths. Serve warm or cold. For storage, do not unwrap. Tamales can be frozen for 6 months or refrigerated for a week. Thaw and boil in water for 30 minutes before serving.

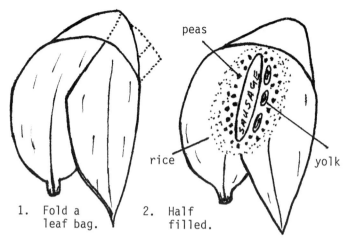

1. Fold a leaf bag.   2. Half filled.

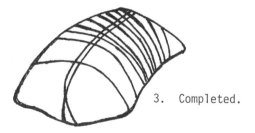

3. Completed.

CHAR SHIU FRIED RICE
makes 9-10 cups

6 cups cooked rice, warm, hot or cold

2 cups diced char shiu, homemade or store bought

6 to 8 water chestnuts (preferably fresh), peeled, rinsed, very finely cut into bits

2 cups diced snow peas, asparagus or tender young green beans

2 green onions, very finely cut into bits

1 to 2 teaspoons sesame oil

1 to 2 tablespoons *each* dark soy sauce and oyster sauce

salt and ground pepper to taste

oil for cooking

Beat together:

      2 eggs

    1/8 teaspoon onion powder

    1/8 teaspoon salt

Heat 1 to 2 tablespoons oil in a preheated wok. Add beaten eggs and make scrambled eggs. Cut into bits with wok spatula while you stir and cook. Remove and set aside.

Add 2 tablespoons oil to wok. When hot, add water chestnuts and snow peas; stir-fry until peas are cooked through, 2 to 2-1/2 minutes. Sprinkle 1 to 2 tablespoons water over vegetables if the wok appears to be dry. Spoon over eggs. Add rice and char shiu to wok; turn and toss until very hot with golden spots here and there. Add soy sauce and oyster sauce; mix. Then, add water chestnuts, snow peas, onions and eggs; mix again. Season with sesame oil, salt and pepper. Mix well and serve hot.

A refreshing soup or simple stir-fried vegetable dish is an ideal choice to accompany fried rice. Fry rice half an hour in advance and keep it hot in a saucepan on stove; wok then will be available for use.

Note. For homemade char shiu, see CANTONESE ROASTED PORK, page 48.

FRIED SWEET RICE
5 to 6 servings

3 cups sweet rice (glutinous rice)

1/4 cup dried shrimp, soaked to soften, picked over

3 links Chinese pork sausage, rinsed and diced

1/4 lb. snow peas

2 oz. canned button mushrooms, drained, diced

1/4 cup finely chopped water chestnuts

1/4 cup finely cut green onion (size of mung beans)

2 tablespoons oyster sauce

salt and/or soy sauce to taste

oil for cooking

Wash and soak rice overnight. Place rice in an 8" fine-mesh colander and make a "well" in the center. Set colander on high rack above water in a large pot. Bring it to a boil; reduce heat and steam 25 to 30 minutes until rice is completely cooked, sprinkling 1/2 cup of cold water over rice during the middle of cooking. While hot, transfer rice to a saucepan and cover to keep it hot.

Pinch off both ends, remove strings and diagonally dice snow peas. Stir-fry snow peas in 1 teaspoon hot oil for 2 minutes or until crisp-tender. Salt to taste. Spoon over rice.

Pan-fry sausages over medium-low heat until golden and cooked through. Scoop out with a slotted spoon and add to rice.

Add shrimp, mushrooms and water chestnuts to pan; stir and cook in sausage oil for 2 minutes. Pour off excess oil. Turn off heat. Add onion, rice, peas, sausages, oyster sauce, salt and soy sauce to taste. Mix well and serve hot.

Fried sweet rice is served on special occasions. It also makes a wonderful stuffing for poultry.

FISH JOOK
(congee)
6 to 10 servings

1-1/4 cups long-grain rice

9 cups water

1 chunk 3/4" thick peeled fresh ginger

1 13-3/4 oz. can clear chicken broth (or beef broth for beef jook)

1 cup green peas, fresh or frozen

1/2 red bell pepper, diced

4 tablespoons minced green onion

2 tablespoons thin soy sauce

2 teaspoons sesame oil

salt and ground pepper to taste

shredded iceberg lettuce

3/4 to 1 lb. fish fillet, completely deboned, thinly sliced (less than 1/8" thick), marinated in:

   1/8 teaspoon *each* ground pepper, ground ginger and garlic powder (minced fresh ginger and garlic may be substituted)

   1/2 teaspoon *each* salt and sesame oil

   2 teaspoons *each* thin soy sauce and sherry

   1 egg, beaten

In a large soup kettle, wash rice several times. Add water, ginger and let soak for 2 hours; then bring to a boil. Reduce heat, cover and simmer 1-1/4 hours. Pick out and discard ginger. Add chicken broth, peas and red pepper. Bring to a boil again. Turn heat to low (gas stove) or off (electric stove). Add fish, then onion, and stir for 1 minute. Season with soy sauce, sesame oil, salt and ground pepper. Ladle soup into bowls; top with lettuce. Serve hot.

Variation #1: Use equal amount of raw shrimp to make shrimp jook. Peel, devein and cut shrimp lengthwise in halves. Marinate as directed.

Variation #2: Use equal amount of thinly sliced chicken meat to make chicken jook. Marinate as directed.

Variation #3: Use equal amount of thinly sliced beef to make beef jook. Marinate beef without egg.

Variation #4: Use equal amount of thinly sliced pork to make pork jook. Marinate as directed and adjust heat to cook pork.

BEEF LO MEIN WITH VEGETABLES
about 6 servings

3/4 lb. dried Chinese war mein (white flat noodles about 1/4" wide) *OR* 12 oz. egg tagliarini, broken into 3 parts

1/2 lb. snow peas (or other vegetables), cut diagonally into 3 or 4 strips

1 small bunch (2 to 3 oz.) Chinese chives or green onions, cut in 1-1/2" lengths

1 clove garlic, crushed

1 to 2 tablespoons *each* oyster sauce and soy sauce

1 to 2 teaspoons sesame oil

oil for cooking   salt   ground pepper

1/2 lb. lean beef, thinly sliced across grain, marinated in:

    1/2 teaspoon beef bouillon powder (optional)

    1/4 teaspoon salt

    pinch ground pepper

    2 teaspoons cornstarch

    1/2 teaspoon *each* sherry and sesame oil

    1 teaspoon *each* dark soy sauce and oil

In a large pot, gradually add noodles to rapidly boiling water. Stir from time to time. Cook only until tender. Do not overcook. Drain, rinse with water, drain again. Mix noodles with 1 tablespoon oil. Cover and keep warm.

Heat wok until hot. Add 1 to 2 tablespoons oil. When oil is hot, brown garlic to extract flavor, then discard garlic. Add beef; stir-fry until half-way cooked. Add chives and continue to stir-fry until the meat has reached the desired doneness. Remove and set aside.

Reheat wok and add 1 tablespoon oil. When hot, stir-fry snow peas with a pinch of salt until peas are crisp-tender, sprinkling 1 to 2 tablespoons of water at a time to create sizzle and steam. Spoon over meat.

Again heat wok and oil it with 1 to 2 tablespoons oil, if needed. Add noodles; stir and toss until hot. Mix in snow peas and meat. Season with salt, pepper, sauces and sesame oil; mix well. Serve as is or with chili oil.

For a meatier one-dish meal, double the stir-fried beef. Stir-fry 1/2 lb. of meat at a time for best flavor and taste.

TOMATO BEEF CHOW MEIN
4 to 6 servings

1   lb. fresh Chinese-style noodles, parboiled only until tender, 2 to 3 minutes, drained and rinsed with cold water, drained again until dry

3   medium tomatoes (1 to 1-1/4 lb.), cut in wedges

1/2   sweet yellow onion, cut in strips

1/2   to 1 green bell pepper, cut in strips (or 1 small bunch Chinese chives, cut in 1" lengths)

1   slice peeled ginger, crushed

1   tablespoon curry powder (optional--for those who like it)

about 1-1/2 tablespoons brown sugar

oil for cooking

salt

3/4   lb. flank steak, thinly sliced (less than 1/8" thick) across the grain, marinated in:

    1/2   teaspoon beef bouillon powder (optional)

    1/2   teaspoon salt

    1/8   teaspoon ground pepper

    1   tablespoon cornstarch

    1/2   teaspoon sesame oil

    1/2   tablespoon *each* sherry, soy sauce and cooking oil

Set wok over high heat until hot. Add 2 tablespoons oil. When hot, add well-drained (and somewhat dry looking) noodles, toss and fry until brown spots appear here and there. As you toss, cut noodles with spatula. Spoon over large platter. Set aside.

Reheat wok. Add 2 to 3 teaspoons oil and a pinch of salt. Stir-fry onion and pepper for 1 to 1-1/2 minutes. Sprinkle 1 to 2 tablespoons water over vegetables if needed. Spoon out and set aside.

Heat wok once more. Add 2 tablespoons oil and ginger; stir until pungent. Add meat; quickly toss to desired doneness, 1-1/2 to 2 minutes. Spoon over onion and pepper. (If chives are used, add chives to beef when the meat is about half-way done.)

Add tomatoes (and optional curry powder) to wok; gently turn and cook to a boil, 1-1/2 to 2 minutes. Add 1/4 teaspoon salt and brown sugar; stir. Turn heat off. Add noodles to wok; mix. Then, add all other remaining ingredients; mix well. Season with more salt or soy sauce (use soy sauce in tomato sparingly!), if needed.

TOSSED NOODLES WITH BEAN SAUCE
6 to 8 servings

2 lb. Chinese-style fresh noodles
1 yellow onion, chopped
oil for cooking
about 1/2 cup chicken broth
more soy sauce or salt, if needed
1 lb. pork butt, minced and marinated in:

    4 teaspoons cornstarch
    2 teaspoons dark soy sauce
    2 teaspoons sherry
    1 teaspoon sesame oil

Combine:

    2 to 3 cloves garlic, minced
    4 tablespoons sweet bean sauce
    2 tablespoons ground bean sauce
    2 tablespoons dark soy sauce
    4 tablespoons chicken broth
    2 teaspoons sesame oil
    3 green onions, minced

Topping: any or all of these
    scallions, shredded
    Chinese chives, cut in 1" lengths
    fresh coriander, cut in 1" pieces
    bean sprouts, stir-fried for 1-1/2 minutes
    shredded carrots
    or your favorite

Cook noodles in rapidly boiling water for 3 minutes. Drain and rinse with water (warm water if you like a warm dish; cold water if you like a cold dish). Drain again, then mix with 1 tablespoon oil. Set aside or keep warm.

Heat wok until hot. Add 2 tablespoons oil. When oil is very hot, add the chopped yellow onion and stir a few times. Do not brown onion. Add pork and stir-fry for 1 to 2 minutes. Add the 1/2 cup chicken broth; cover and simmer until the pork is done. Uncover, add combined sauce ingredients; cook to a boil. Spoon into a serving bowl.

Serve noodles, sauce and topping separately. Let each diner help himself or herself to some noodles, some sauce (as little or as much as desired) and some topping of choice. Or, toss noodles with sauce together and serve the topping on the side.

TOSSED COLD NOODLES
6-8 servings

1 lb. fresh Chinese-style noodles, parboiled 3 minutes, rinsed, drained, mixed with 1/2 tablespoon *each* oil and sesame oil

1/2 to 1 lb. bean sprouts, stir-fried for 1 to 1-1/2 minutes in 1 to 1-1/2 tablespoons hot oil, seasoned with soy sauce and/or salt

1 recipe HOT AND SPICY STIR-FRIED CHICKEN, cooked as directed, page 71

1 or 2 green onions, cut in 1" thin strips

Ginger-Soy Sauce:

1 tablespoon oil

1/4 to 1/3 cup minced preserved Szechwan mustard (not to be confused with preserved mustard green which consists of mostly stems and leaves and is not so spicy; see preserved Szechwan mustard in INGREDIENTS)

1 tablespoon minced peeled ginger

1 tablespoon sesame oil

3 tablespoons dark soy sauce

2 tablespoons chicken broth

1 tablespoon sugar

Serving accompaniment: Let each person sprinkle chili oil over his/her individual dish

Line a large serving platter with noodles, bean sprouts, chicken and green onion in this order.

Heat a heavy small saucepan until hot. Add oil. When hot, add ginger and mustard; stir a few times to mix. Do not brown. Add remaining sauce ingredients; stir and heat through until sugar dissolves. Pour over noodles; toss. Serve with chili oil on the side.

LONG LIFE NOODLE SOUP
6 servings

1 lb. fresh Chinese-style noodles

1/2 lb. pork, thinly sliced across the grain, marinated in:

    1 tablespoon cornstarch

    1/4 teaspoon salt

    dash ground pepper

    1 tablespoon thin soy sauce

Soup:

    1 13-3/4 oz. can clear chicken broth

    3 cups water, more if needed

    2 cups diagonally shredded broccoli or other green vegetable

    salt to taste

Egg Slivers:

    2 eggs

    2 teaspoons water

    pinch of salt

    oil for frying

Beat eggs, salt and water. Coat a 7" pan with oil. When hot, pour 1/4 the egg mixture into pan, tilting to spread over bottom evenly. Bake until top of egg crêpe is set and the underside is golden. Repeat with remaining mixture. Cut crêpes into slivers. Set aside.

Cook noodles in rapidly boiling water, uncovered, until noodles are just tender, about 3 minutes. Pour off hot water; rinse with cold water. Drain.

Bring broth and water to a full boil. Add broccoli and let soup return to a boil. Lower heat. Add pork and stir until cooked through, about 1 minute. Add noodles and season with salt. Top individual servings with egg slivers. Serve immediately.

Long noodles symbolize long life--a "must" treat on birthdays.

HOT AND SOUR NOODLE SOUP
4 to 6 servings

1/2 lb. fresh noodles (1/4" wide, flat war mein type of noodles), cut in manageable lengths

1 roasted chicken breast, skinned, boned, shredded (or 1 to 1-1/2 cups shredded char shiu, see CANTONESE ROASTED PORK)

1/3 to 1/2 cup shredded bamboo shoots

2 or 3 dried Chinese mushrooms, soaked to soften, destemmed, shredded

4 to 8 oz. green vegetables (such as green cabbage, shredded; snow peas, diagonally cut in strips; green beans, french-cut; or asparagus, diagonally cut in strips)

1 green onion, chopped

1 tablespoon ground bean sauce

2 cups rich chicken broth, homemade or store bought

4 cups water

1 teaspoon Chinese chili powder, more or less to taste

1 tablespoon thin soy sauce

1 to 2 teaspoons sesame oil

3 tablespoons rice vinegar

1/4 teaspoon salt, more or less to taste

oil for cooking

In a large pot, add noodles to rapidly boiling water. Cook, uncovered, 3 minutes. Drain, rinse with cold water. Drain again.

Heat a large heavy-bottomed saucepan until fairly hot. Add 1 to 2 teaspoons oil; stir to coat pan. Then add ground bean sauce; swirl. Scatter in bamboo shoots and mushrooms; mix well. Pour in broth and water; bring to a boil, cover, and cook for 3 minutes. Drop in green vegetables and chili powder; stir. When it boils again, add green onion, soy sauce and noodles. Cook only until heated through and hot. Turn heat off. Mix in meat and season with sesame oil, vinegar and salt. Serve immediately.

This noodle soup is very mildly seasoned. One can make it extra hot by adding more chili powder or hot chili oil. Furthermore, the amount of noodles in proportion to the amount of liquid can be varied according to personal preference. In any event, it is a delicious soup. See photo on page 135.

Hunan-style hot and sour noodle soup is usually made with fresh rice noodles. However, fresh rice noodles in soup may be a little too oily.

WON TON
how to make

1 lb. square won ton skins, see won ton skins in INGREDIENTS

Filling: mix together

- 1/2 lb. medium-sized prawns, shelled, deveined, diced
- 1/2 lb. boneless pork butt, minced
- 3 tablespoons minced green onion
- 1 slice ginger, very finely minced
- 6 tablespoons minced bamboo shoots
- 4 teaspoons cornstarch
- 1/8 teaspoon ground pepper
- 1/2 teaspoon salt
- 1/2 tablespoon thin soy sauce
- 1 teaspoon sesame oil

Lay a won ton skin on counter with a corner pointing toward you. Place 1 to 1-1/2 teaspoons filling near the far corner. Fold this corner over the filling to cover, then roll over once toward you. Grasp filled skin with thumbs and forefingers on each side of filling (thumbs on top side of skin). Bend flaps away from you and filling toward you, making a 90° turn on each side by creasing skin near filling so flaps stay flat. Now lay the flaps over each other, making an X. Moisten crossing with a dab of water (or beaten egg) and pinch to seal tightly. Proceed similarly until filling is all used. Freeze or refrigerate leftover skins. Use won ton in soup or deep-fry for hors d'oeuvres. Makes 40 to 55. For soup, see WON TON WAR MEIN for reference. To fry: Heat oil to 360° F. Fry several at a time until golden and cooked through. Drain on absorbent toweling.

WON TON WAR MEIN
6 servings

1   recipe WON TON, page 149

1/4 lb. dried (war mein type) noodles (regular noodles, fresh or dried, may be substituted), cut in 4" lengths

5   cups homemade stock for soup (or use half water, half commercially prepared chicken broth)

4   fresh mushrooms, sliced

1   to 2 cups green vegetables, such as asparagus, snow peas, bok choy or broccoli, cut into shreds

salt to taste

freshly ground pepper or sesame oil

1/2 chicken breast, skinned, boned, thinly sliced, mixed with:

    a   pinch ground pepper

    1   teaspoon cornstarch

    2   teaspoons thin soy sauce

Cook noodles in rapidly boiling water, uncovered, until just tender, 5 to 6 minutes (fresh noodles take about 3 minutes). Drain. Rinse with cold water. Drain again. Toss noodles once in a while to prevent sticking.

Boil another large pot of water. Drop won ton into boiling water. Stir a few times and cook, uncovered, until dumplings float up to the surface. Continue to cook for 1 to 2 minutes longer or until filling is cooked through. Do not overcook. Drain.

Meanwhile, bring soup to a boil. Add mushrooms and green vegetables. When contents boil again, lower heat, ladle 2 tablespoons soup over chicken meat, mix well, then add to soup. Stir until chicken turns white. Turn heat off or remove soup from heat. Salt to taste.

Add noodles, then won ton, to soup. Gently stir. Serve at once. Sprinkle freshly ground pepper over individual servings.

HONEY JERKY

1-1/2   lb. all lean round beef

1/2   to 3/4 teaspoon salt, depending on personal taste

1/4   to 1/2 teaspoon ground ginger (or 1 teaspoon hot chili powder for spicy jerky)

1   tablespoon *each* thin soy sauce and oyster sauce (or 2 tablespoons thin soy sauce for spicy jerky)

1   tablespoon cream sherry

parchment paper

Honey Glaze: heat until hot before coating

1-1/2   tablespoons *each* honey and thin soy sauce, mixed together

Special order an extra-thick piece of beef. Trim fat. Freeze meat until partially frozen. Slice beef *along* grain as thinly as possible (no thicker than 1/8") into 2"x6" strips. Marinate beef in mixture of salt, ginger, soy sauce, oyster sauce and sherry. Let stand overnight in refrigerator. Drain. Line 2 large shallow pans with parchment paper. Arrange beef slices in a single layer. Place pans in oven. Prop the oven door open with a one-inch crack to allow moisture out. Set oven temperature at the lowest possible (140^0 F. is best). Turn beef slices over and change positions of pans occasionally. When jerky is about half dried, turn oven off and on every 30 minutes or so to keep oven hot. Door may be completely closed during the last half of drying period. The approximate total drying time takes 3 to 4 hours. As the thinner pieces get dry, remove from oven; cover and set aside. Then, coat jerky with glaze. At this point, if there is any jerky left (watch for nibblers!), place it in a clean dry glass jar. Cover with lid. Although it keeps at room temperature for one to two weeks, it is best stored in refrigerator. For proper storage, always handle jerky with clean chopsticks or a pair of tongs, not hands.

FRIED FUN GOR
makes 20 fried savory dumplings

oil for deep-frying

1 recipe PORK AND SHRIMP FILLING, cooked as directed, page 186

Dough:

    1/2 cup *each* wheat starch and glutinous rice flour

    1/4 teaspoon salt

     1 teaspoon shortening or lard

    1/2 cup (approximately) boiling water (must be vigorously boiling; instant tap boiling water will not work)

    glutinous rice flour for dusting

Measure starch, flour, salt and shortening into a small mixing bowl. Quickly pour boiling water into flour while stirring to get a partially cooked dough. Knead until smooth, adding more glutinous rice flour if needed to make a workable soft dough. Generally, a soft and slightly sticky dough is much tastier than a hard and dry non-sticky dough. Keep covered. Lightly dust rolling pin and hands with flour. Shape dough evenly into two 10" long rolls. Cut rolls into 20 1-inch pieces. (It is better to break off one piece of dough at a time. Dough will stay moist and warm longer.)

Roll each piece of dough into a 3" circle. Place 2 teaspoons filling in the center. Fold half of the circle over filling to form a half moon. Tightly seal edges. Pinch or patch cracks and torn spots, if any, to avoid splattering during cooking. Place on flat surface with the seam side straight up and the round smooth side down; gently press fun gor down to help it "sit up straight" on the rounded edge.

Deep-fry dumplings, a few at a time, in 365° F. oil until lightly golden, about 2 minutes. Drain on absorbent toweling. Cooked dumplings can be frozen. Reheat in slow oven until hot and crisp. See photo on page 20.

SAVORY FRIED CRESCENTS
makes 12 crescents

Dough:

  1   cup glutinous rice flour

  1   tablespoon wheat starch

  2   tablespoons sugar

  1   teaspoon oil

  1/4 teaspoon salt

  5-1/2 tablespoons (approximately) water

glutinous rice flour for dusting

Filling:

  1/2 tablespoon cornstarch

  2   tablespoons water

  1   cup minced cooked ham

  4   tablespoons dried shrimp, soaked to
      soften, minced

  2   tablespoons minced green onion

  1/4 teaspoon sesame oil

  1/2 tablespoon thin soy sauce

To make filling: In a small saucepan, blend cornstarch and water and cook until thickened. Stir in remaining ingredients. Set aside to cool.

Mix flour and starch in a small mixing bowl; add oil. In a small saucepan, bring water, sugar and salt to a boil. Pour boiling liquid into flour mixture while stirring to get a partially cooked dough. Knead until smooth, adding more hot water or flour as needed to make a workable soft dough. Cover with dampened cloth and let rest for 5 minutes.

Lightly dust rolling pin and hands with flour. Shape dough evenly into a 12" long roll. Cut roll into 12 1-inch portions. (It is better to break off one piece of dough at a time. Dough will stay moist and warm longer.) Roll each piece of dough into a 3" circle. Place 2 teaspoons filling in the center. Fold half of the circle over filling to form a half moon. Tightly seal and crimp edges. Keep crescents covered with cloth.

Deep-fry crescents, a few at a time, over medium-low heat (about 325° F.) for about 3 minutes. These crescents will have an off-white or beige color when cooked. Turn crescents frequently while frying. Remove with slotted spoon and drain on absorbent paper. Deep-fried pastries can be refrigerated or frozen. Place in warm oven to reheat until soft. See GENERAL HINTS ON DEEP-FRYING for reference. Also, see SWEET DOW SAH GOK for illustrations.

FIN-SHAPED SHIU MAI
makes 20-24 steamed dumplings

Dough:

 2 tablespoons potato starch (may be omitted)

 1 cup wheat starch

 1/4 teaspoon salt

 10 tablespoons (approximately) boiling water

 1 teaspoon lard or shortening

 wheat starch for dusting

Pork and Shrimp Filling: mix together

 1/2 lb. boneless pork butt, minced

 1/2 lb. raw medium-sized prawns, shelled, deveined and diced

 5 or 6 dried Chinese mushrooms, soaked to soften, destemmed, squeezed dry, minced

 10 water chestnuts, minced (or 1/4 cup minced bamboo shoots)

 2 tablespoons cornstarch

 1/2 teaspoon salt

 1/8 teaspoon *each* ground pepper and ground ginger (or minced fresh ginger)

 1 tablespoon *each* oyster sauce and soy sauce (or fish sauce)

 1/2 tablespoon *each* sesame oil and sherry

 1/4 cup minced green onion (Chinese chives or coriander)

Dipping Sauce:

 soy sauce, hot mustard, chili oil or your favorite sauce

Measure both starches and salt into a small mixing bowl. Quickly pour boiling water into starches while stirring to get a partially cooked dough. Add lard and knead until smooth, adding more hot water or wheat starch as needed to make a workable soft dough. Cover and let rest for a few minutes before shaping.

Lightly dust rolling pin and hands with flour. Divide dough into 20 to 24 equal pieces. (It is better to break off a piece at a time; dough will stay warm and moist longer.) Roll each piece into a 3" circle. Place 2 to 3 teaspoons filling in the center. Fold circle in half to form a crescent. Pinch edges to seal. Pinch edges again to thin out evenly. Crease this sealed edge to form pleats. Lightly pinch pleats to keep them in place. Finished dumplings have the appearance of a shark's fin. Arrange dumplings in a single layer, without touching, on well greased steaming trays. Steam over boiling water for 15 to 18 minutes or until cooked. Serve plain or with a dipping sauce. See photo on page 38.

For advance preparation, refrigerate cooked dumplings. Reheat by steaming.

RICE NOODLE ROLLS
makes 8 rolls

Batter: combine ingredients and beat until smooth

    2   cups sifted cake flour
    2   tablespoons oil
    1   teaspoon salt (or to taste)
  1-1/2 cups cold water

Filling: mix together and season to taste

    1   cup minced cooked ham, turkey ham or
        other cooked meat
    4   tablespoons dried shrimp, soaked to
        soften, minced (1/4 to 1/2 lb. cooked
        shrimp may be substituted)
    2   tablespoons thin soy sauce or oyster
        sauce (or 1 tablespoon each)
    4   tablespoons minced green onion or
        Chinese chives

oil for cooking

soy sauce or oyster sauce for dip

Oil an 8" square teflon-coated pan. Give batter a
quick stir. Pour 3 tablespoons batter into pan.
Tilt to coat evenly while pan is floating over hot
water in a 12" or 14" skillet. Before batter is
completely set, sprinkle about 3 tablespoons filling on top and pour 2 to 3 more tablespoons of
batter over. Tilt evenly again. Cover and steam
until cooked, about 3 minutes. Remove pan from
steaming water. Run spatula or chopstick around
sides of pan to loosen noodle; roll up. Place
rolled noodle seam side down on oiled platter.
Repeat until batter is all used. Cut rolls into
6 equal pieces and serve warm with dip.

Rice noodle rolls may be served cold. If refrigerated, steam only to heat through, then serve.
Leftover filling can be added to fried rice.

TARO CAKE
8" square cake

2 lb. taro (1 large), see taro in INGREDIENTS
1-1/2 tablespoons oil
2 teaspoons ground bean sauce
1 cup water, more if needed
salt and pepper to taste

Batter: beat until smooth

1/2 teaspoon salt
1-1/4 cups all-purpose flour
14 tablespoons (halfway between 3/4 and 1 cup) water

Topping: mix together

1/4 teaspoon Chinese 5-spice
1/2 strip Chinese-style preserved dried pork, with skin trimmed off, rinsed and minced
3 links Chinese pork sausage, rinsed and minced
1 tablespoon minced fresh coriander
1 tablespoon oyster sauce

Pare and cut taro into 1/2" chunks. Heat oil in a large saucepan or wok, add bean sauce and quickly stir a few times. Immediately add taro, stirring to coat with mixture of sauce and oil. Add water; cover and cook over medium-low heat for 15 minutes, stirring occasionally, and add more water if needed.

Season with salt and pepper. When cooked, taro should be soft, starchy and waterless.

Gently fold batter and half the topping into the cooked taro, then spread evenly into a well-greased 8" square pan. Lightly press remaining topping on surface. Steam over boiling water for 25 minutes. Cool. Turn out and cut into desired size and shape.

Note. Taro is a starchy tuber and is acrid when raw. It can be irritating to sensitive skin and stinging to taste. When fully cooked, it is delicious and nutritious. Wear rubber gloves while handling.

See photo on page 184.

SAUSAGE TURNIP CAKE
8" square cake

1-3/4 lb. Chinese turnips (white radishes called
     lo bok)

ground pepper   salt   cooking oil

Filling: combine and mix

  1/4 cup dried shrimp, soaked to soften,
       minced

    3 links Chinese pork sausage, rinsed,
       minced

    2 tablespoons minced green onion

    1 tablespoon thin soy sauce

Batter: stir together until smooth

  1-1/4 cups white rice flour (milled from long-
         grain rice)

  1/2 teaspoon salt

  add enough water to the reserved liquid (see
  below) to make 3/4 cup

Peel and shred (use shredder) radishes. Heat 1-1/2
tablespoons oil until hot, add radishes and cook,
covered, until tender, about 10 minutes. Season
with pepper and salt. Drain and reserve liquid.
Combine batter, radish and filling; stir well.
Spread and press evenly into a greased 8" square
pan. Steam over boiling water until done, about
15 minutes. Cool, turn out and cut into 2" squares.
Pan-fry each square until golden brown on both
sides. Serve hot or cold. See photo on page 18.

BACON AND CABBAGE CAKE
8" square cake

1 lb. green cabbage, cut into 2"x1/2" pieces

cooking oil   salt   water   ground pepper

Topping: mix

    8 oz. bacon, crisp-fried and crumbled

  1/4 cup dried shrimp, soaked to soften, minced

    1 teaspoon onion powder

    1 tablespoon thin soy sauce

Batter: beat until smooth

  1-1/4 cups all-purpose flour

  1/2 teaspoon salt

  add enough water to the reserved liquid (see
  below) to make 10 tablespoons

Heat 1-1/2 tablespoons oil until hot, add cabbage
and stir well. Add 1 tablespoon water if needed,
and cook until cabbage is limp, about 4 minutes,
stirring often. Season with salt and pepper. Drain
and reserve liquid. Combine batter, cabbage and
half of the topping; stir well. Spread evenly into
a greased 8" square pan. Gently press on remaining
topping. Steam until wooden pick inserted in center
comes out clean, about 12 minutes. While warm, turn
out, cut and serve.

PAN-FRIED TURNIP CAKES
makes 10 mini cakes

oil for pan-frying

Dough:

    1-1/2   cups all-purpose flour

    1/2   teaspoon salt

    1/4   cup shortening

    3   tablespoons + 1 teaspoon cold water (add another 1/2 teaspoon, if needed)

Filling:

    1-1/2   links Chinese pork sausage, steamed for 10-12 minutes, finely ground

    1   lb. Chinese white radishes (white turnips), or jicama or Japanese daikon radish

    1/2   whole green onion, minced

    a   pinch ground white pepper

    1/8   teaspoon salt or to taste (make it slightly on the salty side with radish filling)

    1/4   teaspoon *each* thin soy sauce and sesame oil

Peel radishes or jicama, then shred with shredder. Cook in its own juice with a pinch of salt and 1/2 teaspoon oil until wilted and cooked through. Cool. Squeeze out all juice. Save juice for cooking other vegetables. Mix all filling ingredients together. Set aside. This part can be done in advance and kept in refrigerator.

In a small mixing bowl, combine flour, salt and shortening. Cut with two knives or pastry blender until shortening is finely cut into flour. Gradually add water while mixing to form dough similar to pie dough. Dough should be slightly on the dry side. Divide dough into 10 equal parts.

Take a portion of dough and roll it out into a 4" circle. Dot the center with 1 tablespoon filling. Gather edges to enclose filling. While twisting to insure a secure seal, flatten to form a 2" round flat mini cake. Twist off any excess dough at the seams. Place on platter with seam side down. Proceed until all 10 mini cakes are made. See photo on page 18.

Heat 1/2 to 1 cup of oil in a wok (wok is best; it uses the least amount of oil) until hot. Add 4 or 5 cakes at a time, and pan-fry over medium to medium-high heat until both sides are golden brown and cooked through, about 4 minutes. Drain cakes on absorbent toweling. Serve hot or cold for dim sum.

REAL CRUNCHY ONION PANCAKES
makes 7 pancakes

4 to 5 green onions, minced (cut onions finely
    for best appearance; do not mince in food
    processor or chop)

cooking oil   sesame oil   salt

Dough:

      2 cups sifted all-purpose flour

    1/4 teaspoon salt

    3/4 cup boiling water

      1 tablespoon cold water, more if needed

    all-purpose flour for dusting

Paste:

      3 tablespoons cornstarch

      2 tablespoons cold water

    about 1 cup boiling water, more if needed

Measure flour and salt into mixing bowl. Gradually
add boiling water while stirring. Add cold water
and stir well to form a non-sticky soft dough.
Turn out onto lightly floured surface; knead only
until smooth. Cover with dampened towel and let
rest for 15 minutes.

Divide dough into 14 equal portions. Roll into
balls. Lightly flour rolling pin and board. (Use
as little dry flour for dusting as possible.)

Flatten a ball to a 3" circle and thoroughly brush
the top and edge with oil. Flatten a second ball
to a 3" circle and place it over the oiled circle--
sandwich style. Roll out the "sandwich" into a 6"
circle. Set aside on a piece of waxed paper for
easier handling and stacking; cover with dampened
towel. Proceed similarly with remaining dough.

Over medium-low to medium heat, heat an ungreased
but well-seasoned flat-bottomed pan until hot. Remove a "sandwich" and put into pan. Wait for 20
seconds or until it becomes non-stick, then turn
over. Wait for 20 seconds, then rotate "sandwich"
quickly with hand or chopsticks until small golden
spots barely become visible on the bottom. Turn
over and rotate as above to cook the other side
in the same manner. Do not permit pancakes to
brown. Remove from pan, separate "sandwich" into
single pancakes and stack on platter. Cover with
towel until ready to proceed. These pancakes, at
this stage, are called Mandarin pancakes and are
served with Peking duck or *mo shu pork*. For advance preparation, refrigerate well-wrapped pancakes.

To make the paste: Mix cornstarch with cold water

in a narrow deep bowl. Pour boiling water into this mixture while stirring to make 1 to 1-1/8 cups of cooked thick paste.

Spread two pancakes on counter. Brush tops with paste, adding 2 or 3 drops of sesame oil if you wish. Generously sprinkle with salt on both pancakes, (generally, pancakes will have a better flavor if they are slightly salty) and sprinkle about 1 tablespoon green onion on one pancake. Place both pancakes together to make a "sandwich" with the sticky sides together. Press "sandwich" with hand to align pancakes, especially the edges. It is important that the edges adhere to seal in the filling.

Heat oil to about 360° F. Deep-fry "sandwiches", one at a time (unless you are using a very large wok), until crisp and evenly golden, turning pancakes over frequently. Do not allow pancakes to turn dark brown or burn. Adjust oil temperature accordingly. Stand fried pancake on its side to drain the oil.

Serve pancakes whole or cut pancakes into wedges, pizza-style. Eat out of hand. Serve as appetizers, snacks or party food. Crisp and delicious! No one can stop with just one slice!

This recipe may seem time consuming, but the actual work goes quite fast. The resulting pancakes are worth the effort. For Mandarin pancakes, roll out "sandwich" (in second paragraph) to as thin as possible. For convenience, use beaten eggs in place of cooked thick paste.

LAYERED FLAKY BAKING PASTRY DOUGH
makes 10 buns

Dough A:

      2   cups all-purpose flour
    1/3   cup vegetable shortening
      1   tablespoon sugar
    1/8   teaspoon salt
  5-1/3   tablespoons (approximately) ice water

Dough B:

      1   cup all-purpose flour
    1/4   cup lard
  2-1/2   teaspoons (approximately) ice water

To make dough A: Measure flour, shortening, sugar and salt into mixing bowl. Blend with pastry blender until fine. Gradually add water and continue to blend until dough will hold together (similar to pie dough). *Do not overwork dough.*

Repeat the above procedure with dough B. Dough B should be somewhat dry and crumbly.

Divide each dough into 10 equal portions. Flatten a piece of dough A. Place a portion of dough B in the center and wrap around with dough A to form a ball. Roll out on smooth surface to a 5"x8" rectangle. Then, starting with a short side, roll up into a 5" stick. Turn stick so that one end points toward you, and roll out into a rectangle of approximately 2"x8". Starting with a narrow end, fold up to get a 4-layered square. Keep covered. Repeat until all the squares are made. Now, the flaky pastry dough is ready to be rolled out into circles for filling.

The best way to roll out the dough is to: Roll out 2 or 3 times, turn dough over; roll out 2 or 3 times and turn dough over; etc. The dough rolls out much easier, resulting in flakier crust.

This is the all-purpose flaky pastry dough. After rolling each square into a 5-1/2" to 6" circle, it may then be stuffed with any savory filling or sweet filling (such as lotus nut paste or red bean paste), and made into any pastry shape. See SO BAO recipe for reference. (Note. For extra-light crust, use 1/2 cup shortening with 3 to 3-1/2 tablespoons ice water in dough A.)

SO BAO
makes 10 baked flaky buns

1 recipe LAYERED FLAKY BAKING PASTRY DOUGH,
   page 162

1 recipe ROASTED PORK FILLING, page 185;
   or 1 recipe CHILI-FLAVORED PORK FILLING,
   page 185

1 egg yolk, beaten with 1/2 teaspoon water and
   1/4 teaspoon dark soy sauce

white sesame seeds

parchment paper, cut in 10 circles of 2-1/2" in
   diameter

Prepare filling and dough as directed. Take a
square of dough and roll it out into a 5-1/2" to
6" circle, thinning the edges more than the center.
Pleat around dough to form a deep cup and pinch
pleats to keep them in shape. Place 1-1/2 to 2
tablespoons filling in the center. Enclose filling by squeezing bun with palm of one hand and
gathering edges with fingers of the other hand.
Twist gathered edges to seal securely, and twist
off any excess dough at top. Brush top and sides
with yolk mixture and sprinkle sesame seeds over
bun. Set bun on a parchment paper, then place on
baking sheet. Repeat until all buns are made.

Bake at 350° F. until golden or until done, about

35 minutes. Serve warm or cold. If buns were filled
with roasted pork filling, they make the best *char
shiu bao*. See HONEY CHAR SHIU BAO for comparison.

So bao freezes well. Reheat in slow oven and serve
warm. Keep some on hand for unexpected company.

See second photo on page 28.

HONEY CHAR SHIU BAO
makes 18 baked pork buns

Dough:

    1   packet active dry yeast

    1   cup warm water (105° to 115° F.)

  1/4 teaspoon salt

  1/3 cup sugar

    1   large egg yolk and 1 large whole egg

    3   tablespoons melted shortening

4-1/4 cups (plus or minus 2 tablespoons) all-purpose flour

all-purpose flour for dusting

Char Shiu Filling:

    1   lb. coarsely minced char shiu, homemade (see CANTONESE ROASTED PORK) or store bought

  3/4 to 1 cup (1 medium) chopped onion (sweet yellow onion)

    2   tablespoons oyster sauce

  1/8 teaspoon ground pepper

    2   tablespoons oil

Thickener: mix

        1   tablespoon cornstarch

        6   tablespoons water, more if needed

Honey Glaze: mix

    1   tablespoon honey

    1   tablespoon warm water

Dissolve yeast in warm water. Beat eggs with sugar and salt. Gradually add dissolved yeast, shortening and half the flour, beating until smooth. By hand, stir in remaining flour. Let rest for 5 minutes. Turn out onto lightly floured surface; knead until elastic and smooth. Place dough in a greased bowl, cover with towel and let rise in warm place until dough is at least doubled, 1-1/2 to 2 hours. Punch down, cover and let rest a few minutes.

To cook filling: Stir-fry onion in 2 tablespoons hot oil until limp. Add thickener; stir until bubbly. Add meat, oyster sauce and pepper; mix well. Cool. Filling may be prepared in advance.

Dust hands with flour. Shape dough evenly into two 9" long rolls. Cut rolls into 18 one-inch pieces. Stretch a piece of dough into a 4" circle and dot the center with 2 tablespoons filling. Gather edges to enclose filling, then roll into a ball. Place bun in well-greased muffin tin. Repeat until all buns are made. Cover with cloth; let rise until the dough is almost doubled, 20-30 minutes. Bake in a preheated 350° F. oven until golden, about 20 minutes. Brush top with honey mixture, then remove buns from muffin pans. Serve hot or cold. This dough also makes wonderful plain dinner rolls. See page 202.

164

COILED SAUSAGE BUNS
makes 20 steamed buns

1 pair (2 links) Chinese pork sausage, steamed for 10-12 minutes, finely ground; reserve 1 tablespoon for garnish

20 2-1/2" square (or round) parchment papers

Steamed Bun Dough:

2-3/4 teaspoons or 1 packet dry yeast

1 cup + 1 tablespoon warm water, 105°-115° F.

3/4 teaspoon salt

1/2 cup sugar

2 tablespoons melted shortening

1 cup white rice flour, see white rice flour in INGREDIENTS

3 cups all-purpose flour

all-purpose flour for dusting

Add a tablespoon of the measured sugar to the dry yeast; stir. Add water to yeast mixture; blend. When the yeast and sugar have dissolved completely, add shortening. Combine flour, salt and remaining sugar in a large bowl and stir a few times to mix. Gradually pour yeast mixture into flour mixture while stirring to form a dough. Let rest 5 minutes. Turn out onto lightly floured surface. Knead until smooth and elastic. Place dough in a greased bowl, cover with dampened towel and let rise in warm place until dough is at least doubled (you should get one large mixing bowl full), 1-1/2 to 2 hours. Punch down, cover and let rest a few minutes before shaping.

Divide dough into 2 equal parts. Roll out dough, one part at a time, into 12"x14" rectangle. Spread half the ground sausage over top. Starting with a 14-inch edge, fold up into a 4-layered 14" long "jelly roll". Gently press and stretch "jelly roll", so filling will adhere to dough. Cut "jelly roll", crosswise, into 3/8" (or less, but not any wider) strips. As you slice, stretch the "jelly roll" in either direction to tailor cutting. Mentally divide strips into 10 equal bunches. Take a bunch of dough strips (usually about 6 strips), holding one end in each hand, and stretch the strips to 6" long. Wind strips around index and middle fingers while stretching with other hand. When winding has completed, you have a "snail" or "coil" shaped bun. Tuck in ends. Garnish top with bits of sausage and set bun on a piece of paper. It is best to wind bun somewhat like a cone so it won't tilt and become a leaning tower. Cover with cloth and let rise for 15 to 20 minutes or until the dough is light. Steam to cook, 10-12 minutes. Serve. Steamed buns freeze well. Reheat by steaming. Great for dim sum, snacks, luncheon and dinner. See photo on page 31.

SILVER-THREAD SAUSAGE ROLLS
makes 20 steamed buns

1   recipe Steam Bun Dough, page 165

5   links Chinese pork (or liver) sausage, rinsed, steamed for 10-12 minutes; cut each link in fourths

20 2-1/2" square or round parchment papers

Filling:

    4 teaspoons melted (or very soft) shortening

    4 teaspoons granulated sugar

Prepare dough as directed. After the first rising, divide dough in half. Roll out each half into a 12" by 14" rectangle. Spread 1 to 2 teaspoons shortening over dough, then sprinkle 1 to 2 teaspoons sugar on top. Starting with a 14" edge, fold up into a 14" long 4-layered "jelly roll". Gently press and stretch "jelly roll" so sugar will adhere to dough. Slice "jelly roll", crosswise, into 3/8" (or less, but not any wider) strips. As you slice, stretch the "jelly roll" in either direction to tailor your cutting. Mentally divide strips into 10 parts, about 6 strips in each part. Take a bunch of about 6 strips, holding one end in each hand, stretch strips to 5" to 6" in length, then wrap dough around a piece of sausage. Tuck in ends. Place bun on paper with seam side down. Proceed until all buns are made. Cover with cloth and let rise in a warm place until dough is light, 15 to 20 minutes. Steam for 10-12 minutes. Serve hot or cold. These silver-thread sausage rolls are most attractive and can be refrigerated or frozen. Reheat by steaming.

Variation #1: Omit sausage. Take a bunch of 6 dough strips. Even out or tuck in ends. Place on paper. Cover, let rise and steam as directed. These dinner rolls have the appearance of the familiar "flaky gem dinner rolls".

Variation #2: Make plain steamed buns to serve with Peking duck. After first rising, divide dough into 20 portions. Simply roll a portion of dough into a ball, place on parchment paper, let rise, and steam as directed above.

See photo on page 38.

RICE MEAT BALLS
makes about 30 rice meat balls

3/4 cup glutinous (sweet) rice, washed, soaked overnight, drained until dry, mixed with 1 to 2 tablespoons all-purpose flour

Filling: mix together

1/2 lb. fresh (not frozen) ground pork, preferably chopped with cleaver so meat is succulent and adhesive

1/2 lb. raw medium-sized prawns, shelled, deveined and coarsely minced (or finely diced)

3 large dried Chinese mushrooms, soaked to soften, destemmed, squeezed dry, minced

5 water chestnuts, well minced

2 tablespoons cornstarch

1/2 scant teaspoon salt

1/8 teaspoon *each* ground ginger (or minced fresh ginger) and pepper

1 tablespoon *each* oyster sauce and soy sauce

1 teaspoon *each* sesame oil and sherry

2 to 3 tablespoons minced green onion, Chinese chives or coriander

Oil hands. Roll the sticky meat mixture into balls about the size of a small walnut. Then roll the meat balls in rice to completely cover the meat. Remove any grains that are not sticking to meat. Place rice meat balls on well-greased metal steam-ing trays. (Do not use plates.) Steam above boiling water until cooked through, 15 to 20 minutes. For perfect appearance and easy removal, cool 5 minutes, then serve. Good for appetizer or dim sum.

Leftover rice, if any, can be added to long-grain rice and cooked for dinner. To insure success, rice and filling should be at room temperature. Chilled rice and/or filling may not adhere.

CHINESE SPRING ROLLS
makes 10 rolls

square lumpia wrappers, see lumpia wrappers in
   INGREDIENTS

oil for deep-frying

sweet and sour sauce or chili oil for dip

Filling:

  1/2 lb. char shiu (see CANTONESE ROASTED PORK),
       cut in shreds

    6 oz. green cabbage, pat very dry, shredded

  1/2 red bell pepper, shredded (or 1 medium
       carrot, peeled, then shaved into shreds
       with potato peeler)

mix:

  1/2 teaspoon sugar

    2 teaspoons cornstarch

    1 tablespoon thin soy sauce

    2 tablespoons water

Paste: mix

    1 tablespoon all-purpose flour

  2-1/2 to 2-3/4 teaspoons water

To cook filling: Heat wok until very hot. Add 1
to 1-1/2 tablespoons oil; swirl to coat wok. Add
pepper and cabbage and stir-fry as fast as you can
for 2 minutes. Sprinkle a tablespoon of water over
vegetables to create sizzle and steam, and to prevent burning. Cabbage should be just limp, crunchy
and waterless. Add sauce around sides of wok; quickly mix and stir until thickened. Remove from heat
and mix in meat. Spoon into dish. Filling should
be waterless, slightly slippery and sticky to touch.

Spread a wrapper on kitchen counter with a corner
pointing toward you, and lay a strip of filling
across center of wrapper. Starting from the corner
nearest you, fold it over the filling, then roll
over once. Moisten left and right corners with
paste, then fold in both corners. Roll up and moisten the last corner to seal. Deep-fry in 365° F.
oil until golden brown, 1 to 2 minutes, rolling frequently. Drain on racks. Cut each roll in fourths.
While hot and crisp, serve plain or with dip.

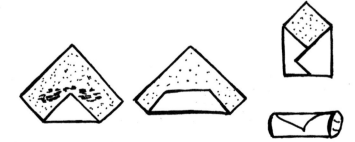

CHINESE CABBAGE ROLLS
10-12 rolls

10 to 12 large whole napa cabbage leaves, dipped in boiling water for 1-1/2 to 2 minutes, rinsed with cold water, well-drained

1 large roasted chicken breast, boned, cut in shreds

1/2 lb. cooked ham, cut in thin shreds

1 green onion, cut in 1" thin shreds

5 or 6 large fresh mushrooms, sliced

1 10-3/4 oz. can cream of mushroom soup, stirred

Sauce: mix well and cook to a boil

    2 teaspoons cornstarch

    2 teaspoons curry powder

    1 cup chicken broth

    1 teaspoon sesame oil

    remaining mushroom soup from above

    soy sauce or salt to taste

Heat wok until hot. Add 1 tablespoon oil and a pinch of salt. Stir-fry mushrooms until heated through, 2 minutes. Add chicken, ham, 2/3 of the mushroom soup and onion. Mix well. Add 1 to 2 tablespoons of water if needed to make a moist filling. Season with ground pepper to taste.

Lay a cabbage leaf on counter. Fill the leafy portion with 1/10 (or 1/12) of filling. Roll up and tuck in ends. Place cabbage roll, seam side down, on lightly oiled roasting pan (about the size of a 10" cake pan). Proceed until all rolls are made.

Prepare sauce as directed, then pour over cabbage rolls. Bake in 350° F. oven to heat through. Serve at once.

DEEP-FRIED HAR KOW
makes 20 shrimp balls

oil for deep-frying

2 to 3 tablespoons cornstarch for dredging

sweet and sour sauce, mustard or chili oil for dip

Mix together:

- 1/2 lb. medium-sized prawns, shelled, deveined, coarsely minced (about 3/4 cup)

- 1/4 lb. pork (not too lean, not too fat), preferably finely minced with cleaver

- 2 dried Chinese mushrooms, soaked, destemmed, finely minced (or 2 to 3 tablespoons well-minced bamboo shoot)

- 1 slice peeled ginger, very finely minced

- 1/2 green onion, finely cut into bits (size of green mung beans)

- 1 egg (large) white, beaten

- 1/4 teaspoon salt

- 4 teaspoons cornstarch

- 1 teaspoon *each* sherry, sesame oil and thin soy sauce

For ease of handling, chill shrimp mixture. Divide mixture into 20 equal parts. Shape each into a ball. Dredge balls with cornstarch. Deep-fry, a few at a time, in 340° to 350° F. oil until golden and cooked through, 3 to 4 minutes. Drain on racks. Serve with dip.

CRISP GLUTINOUS RICE PACKETS
make as many as desired

1 recipe FRIED SWEET RICE, cooled, page 141

square lumpia wrappers, see lumpia wrappers in INGREDIENTS

oil for deep-frying

Paste: mix as much as needed in the following proportion

- 1 tablespoon all-purpose flour
- 2-1/2 to 2-3/4 teaspoons water

Lay a wrapper on counter with a corner pointing toward you. Spread 4 to 5 tablespoons rice filling across center of wrapper. Starting from the corner nearest you, fold it over the filling and roll over once. Moisten left and right corners with paste, then fold in both corners. Roll up and moisten the last corner to seal. Be sure all seams are tightly sealed. Place on flat surface with seam side down. Wrap as many as desired. Deep-fry packets, a few at a time, in 365° to 375° F. oil until golden and crisp, about 2 minutes, turning frequently. The oil temperature and frying time depend on the type of wrapper used. Test the oil temperature with a wrapper. It should be sizzling hot without burning within the first minute. Drain packets on racks. Serve packets whole, halved, or in thirds. Soy sauce may be used as dip.

BOK TONG GO
sweet rice cake-pudding

Batter:

- 1/2 cup extra-fancy long-grain rice
- 10 tablespoons sugar
- 1/2 cup water
- 1 tablespoon melted shortening for softer texture, or omit shortening for a chewier texture

Leavening Agent:

- 1/2 teaspoon sugar from above measured sugar
- 1/2 teaspoon active dry yeast
- 2 tablespoons warm water

Paste:

- 1 tablespoon batter from above, see below
- 3 tablespoons hot water

Bok tong go, white sugar cake-pudding, in English translation, is extremely difficult to make. Its ingredients are few, but the technique of producing its sweet, spongy, snow white, light, chewy and smooth texture requires a professional touch. Unlike sponge cakes, the cut sides of *bok tong go* display "vertical long air pockets". Every step must be followed precisely to yield the perfect result.

Start with the freshest ingredients. Rice that has been purchased and stored for a long time may have lost most of the natural moisture and oil which are essential for success. Sugar should be lump-free and yeast must be active.

Rinse rice several times or until water is clear. Soak rice with plenty of water for 40 to 48 hours. For summer days or where climate is hot, change water once or twice to preserve freshness.

To make batter: Measure water into blender (food processor will not do this task well). Add well-drained rice. Cover and start grinding at low speed for 1 minute. Switch to high speed to liquefy rice. Gradually add sugar and shortening. Occasionally stop the motor to shake the contents or scrape the sides of bowl with rubber spatula. This liquefying process takes approximately 10 minutes. Be sure to have a sharp blender blade for this job. Pour batter through a fine-meshed strainer placed over a small mixing bowl. There should be no residue.

While blender is in operation, mix leavening agent.

Use only warm (about 105° F.) water; hot water will kill the yeast. Set aside.

To make the paste: Pour hot water into a heavy-bottomed small saucepan. Add the 1 tablespoon prepared batter. Constantly stir mixture over medium heat and cook to a thickened smooth white paste similar to white glue. Remove from heat.

Add 1 tablespoon batter to paste; stir to blend. Add a second tablespoon batter to paste; stir to blend. Add a third tablespoon batter to paste and stir to blend. Then pour paste into batter; stir to blend. By this time, yeast may have doubled its volume. Check the temperature of batter. If it is just warm, add yeast mixture and blend well. If hot (metal base and glass bowl of blender conduct heat; batter may get quite hot), wait until warm, then add yeast. Cover batter with cloth and set in a draft-free warm place (a preheated warm oven works well in the winter) to rise.

Fermentation generally takes 2-1/2 to 3 hours. Depending on the weather and temperature of kitchen. (Occasionally, 2 hours will be sufficient. Experience will be the best teacher!) Stir batter after 1 hour. Let rise for another hour, then stir again. If batter is very bubbly and can not be easily stirred down, let rise for another 30 minutes, then steam. Otherwise, let it rise for 1 more hour. Fermentation period should not exceed 3 hours as yeast uses up sugar, causing a sour taste and unpleasant odor.

Set a 9" (or equivalent) non-stick pan on steaming rack in a large pot or steamer. When water is about to reach the boiling point, give batter a gentle stir (do not completely stir it down) and pour into pan. Cover and steam (between medium-high and high heat is best) until done, about 10 minutes. Remove pan from heat. Cool pudding thoroughly. For a glossy appearance, smooth a little oil over the surface before cutting with oiled sharp knife. Serve for snacks, dim sum lunch or dessert. Do not freeze leftovers. Wrap well, then refrigerate or keep at room temperature (in the winter) overnight. To reheat, steam over gently boiling water only to heat through.

Important. Do not double recipe by doubling ingredients. Do one recipe at a time.

BOK TONG GO

SANDWICH POCKETS

SANDWICH POCKETS
makes 20

20 slices fresh soft white bread
 1 recipe PORK AND SHRIMP FILLING, cooked as directed, page 186
 2 egg yolks, beaten
oil for deep-frying

Trim bread crust, then roll out with rolling pin into a thin square. Fill each square with a heaping table-spoon filling. Diagonally fold in half. Moisten edges with yolk and very firmly pinch to seal. Trim edges to a perfect triangle if needed.

Deep-fry pockets in 365° F. oil until golden, 30 to 60 seconds. Drain. Serve while hot and crisp.

Variation: Fold in half crosswise and seal to make "sandwich pillows".

Note. It is not necessary to roll out the bread; sealing is easier and the taste is crunchier. However, rolled bread gives a smoother appearance and absorbs less oil. For advance preparation, make pockets 2 to 4 hours ahead, then deep-fry just before serving.

CRUNCHY ALMOND COOKIES
makes 3 dozen

1/2   cup lard (no substitutes)

3/4   cup sugar

1/8   teaspoon salt

 1   large egg

 1   teaspoon dark soy sauce* (regular black
      soy sauce)

1/2   teaspoon almond extract

 2   cups sifted all-purpose flour

1/2   teaspoon baking soda

1/2   teaspoon baking powder

almond halves

Glaze:

> 1   egg yolk
>
> 1/2 teaspoon water
>
> orange food color, paste or liquid (can be
> omitted)

To make glaze: Stir egg yolk and water until well blended. Gradually add orange food color (by the tip of a toothpick if using paste color; by the drop if using liquid color) while stirring to obtain a deep orange color. Set aside.

Combine lard, sugar, salt and egg in mixing bowl; beat well. Add soy sauce and almond extract; blend.

Mix together flour, baking soda and baking powder. Stir in flour mixture. Chill dough for 30 minutes. Shape dough into size of small walnuts and place on shallow baking pans or cookie sheets. Allow 1-1/2" space between cookies. Slightly flatten cookies and press a shallow depression down centers of cookies. As soon as the first pan is filled, put it in the refrigerator. Make remaining cookies and place this pan in refrigerator also.

Take the first pan out of refrigerator. Lightly brush cookies with yolk mixture, being careful not to fill the depressions with yolk. Press an almond half onto each center. Return these cookies to refrigerator. Similarly, do the finishing touches on cookies in the second pan. Chill for an hour.

Bake in preheated 300^{0} F. oven for about 20 minutes. Cookies should have a beautiful golden brown (not brown or burned) color on the bottom and should be crunchy to taste when cooled. Cool cookies on racks. Store in airtight container. See page 16.

* One teaspoon dark soy sauce adds a nice color without any soy sauce flavor.

SESAME COOKIES
makes 6 dozen

1/4 cup margarine
1/2 cup lard
3/4 cup sugar
1/8 teaspoon salt
  1 medium egg
  1 teaspoon dark soy sauce (regular black soy)
1/2 teaspoon vanilla
2-1/4 cups sifted all-purpose flour
  1 teaspoon baking powder
1/4 teaspoon baking soda
white sesame seeds, toasted to a pale gold

Combine margarine, lard, sugar, salt and egg in
mixing bowl; beat well. Add soy sauce and vanilla;
blend. Mix together flour, baking soda and baking
powder. Stir in flour mixture. Chill dough for
30 minutes. Shape dough in nickel-sized round balls,
roll in sesame seeds, and place on shallow baking
pans (shallow baking pans protect cookies from browning too fast) or cookie sheets. Allow 1-1/2" space
between cookies. Place cookies in refrigerator to
chill for an hour.

Bake in preheated 300° F. oven for about 20 minutes
or until golden brown on the bottom and the entire

cookie is cooked through. In other words, our aim
is to bake the cookies so that they are crisp through
(when cooled) without browning them too much. This
means low heat and longer baking time. If necessary,
turn heat off and leave cookies in oven for 3 to 4
minutes longer, and/or change the position of cookie
sheet to get an even golden color. Cookies should
have a beautiful golden brown color (similar to golden
brown sugar) on the bottom. When cooled, cookies
will have a crunchy texture. Underbaked cookies will
have a soft and chewy center. Thoroughly cool cookies,
then store in airtight container.

GINGER COOKIES
makes 4 dozen

1/2   cup (1 stick) *each* butter and margarine,
      at room temperature
1/2   cup granulated sugar
2   cups all-purpose flour
1/4   cup finely minced crystallized ginger
      (4 good slices)
1   cup chopped walnuts

Cream butter, margarine and sugar until light.
Stir in flour, ginger and walnuts. Drop dough,
by the tablespoonful, onto shallow baking pans.
(Shallow baking pans are best for baking cookies;
the sides of pan will help to keep cookies from
burning.) Refrigerate until firm. Roll each
into a ball, then lightly flatten. (May be
refrigerated for 2 to 3 hours, then bake.)

Bake in preheated 350° F. oven until cooked
through and lightly golden on the bottom. Do not
overbake or allow cookies to turn dark brown.
Check for doneness after 15 minutes. Generally,
it is better to bake cookies longer at a lower
temperature. High temperature can result in
burned and raw cookies. Cool cookies on racks
before storage.

SESAME-PEANUT SOUP
2 or 3 servings

1/4   cup unsalted dry-roasted peanuts
2   tablespoons toasted white sesame seeds (toast
      in a slow oven or in an ungreased skillet over
      burner set on low heat)
1   cup water
1/4   cup sugar
3   tablespoons evaporated milk

Mix:
2   teaspoons cornstarch
1   tablespoon water

In blender, grind peanuts, sesame seeds with 1/2 cup
water until liquefied. Strain (optional) into a
heavy-bottomed saucepan; discard residue. Add sugar
and the remaining 1/2 cup water. Bring to a boil,
stirring often. Thicken with cornstarch mixture
and cook until bubbly. Remove from heat. Mix in
milk.

Sesame-peanut soup is a delicious dessert.

GLAZED APPLES
4 servings

2   apples (red delicious or pippin), peeled, cored, cut (each) in 6 wedges

2   teaspoons toasted white sesame seeds

2   tablespoons cornstarch for dusting

oil for deep-frying

Batter: mix until smooth

    5   tablespoons cornstarch

    3   tablespoons all-purpose flour

    1   extra large egg

    1   tablespoon water

Syrup:

    1/3   cup sugar

    3   tablespoons white corn syrup

Lightly oil a serving platter; set aside. Heat oil to 350° to 360° F. Dust apple wedges with cornstarch, then dip into batter. Lift up to allow excess batter to drip back into bowl. Deep-fry coated apple wedges over medium-low heat until golden, 3 to 4 minutes. When apple is cooked, juice begins to drip, causing oil to splatter. This is an indication of doneness. Oil must be hot enough so it sizzles when apple is dropped into it. On the other hand, apple wedges must be cooked through with a pale gold crust. Adjust heat accordingly. Remove the pieces to drain. If desired, deep-fry a second time for about 30 seconds just before coating with syrup.

Heat sugar and corn syrup in a heavy medium saucepan over medium to medium-high heat. When syrup has thickened to the "advanced soft ball stage", turn heat off; leave saucepan on stove to keep it hot. Add fried apples. Quickly but gently toss and mix to coat evenly. Spread glazed apples on platter. Sprinkle sesame seeds on top. Serve at once. When cooled at room temperature, the syrup coating is not hardened and can still make "sugar threads" when pulled apart.

Variations: Omit sesame seeds. Let each diner plunge a piece of syrup-coated apple into ice-cold water for a few seconds to harden syrup, then eat. OR, pour 2 to 3 tablespoons brandy (flaming rum or cognac) over syrup-coated apples and ignite it to flame. Then dip each piece in ice-cold water and serve. This makes an impressive presentation, but you must be able to work fast. For a delightful change, substitute 2 or 3 firm-ripe bananas for apples. Proceed as directed above. Deep-fry until pale gold and cooked through, 2 to 3 minutes. This is an elegant dessert to conclude any meal.

CRUNCHY SESAME BOW TIES
makes 40 cookies

1   tablespoon lard

1   medium egg, at room temperature

1/4   cup sugar

1   cup all-purpose flour

1   to 1-1/2 teaspoons black sesame seeds, picked over

1   large sheet waxed paper, 25-26 inches long (for easy removal of thin dough)

all-purpose flour for dusting

Stir lard, egg and sugar until well blended. Mix in flour and sesame seeds; stir well to form a dough similar to pie crust dough. Cover with towel and let rest for 15 minutes.

Lightly dust waxed paper and rolling pin with flour. Place dough on waxed paper and roll it out into a 12"x15" rectangle. (Beginners may roll dough to a smaller size, but not less than 12"x12". Dough must be thin enough to give crunchiness.) Cut lengthwise into eight 1-1/2" strips; that is, cut at 1-1/2" intervals to obtain eight 15-inch-long strips. Then cut crosswise at 3" intervals. You now have a total of forty 1-1/2"x3" rectangles. Take one small rectangle, cut a 2" lengthwise slit in the center, leaving 1/2" uncut edge at each end.

Pull one end of rectangle through slit to resemble a "bow tie". Make all 40 "bow ties". Deep-fry "bow ties", several at a time, in 365° F. oil until golden. Drain on toweling. Cool thoroughly. Serve or store in airtight container. For variations: Before serving, sprinkle with a mixture of powdered sugar and cinnamon; or coat them with a sticky syrup.

178

ALMOND CURD
6 servings

Almond Curd:

 1   package unflavored gelatin

 5   tablespoons sugar

 1   cup boiling water for firmer curd or 1-1/2 cups boiling water for softer curd

1/2   cup fresh milk

1/2   teaspoon almond extract

Syrup:

1/3   cup sugar

 2   cups water

 2   tablespoons almond powder mixed with 2 tablespoons water

1/4   to 1/2 teaspoon almond extract

canned Mandarin orange sections or fresh orange sections cut into small pieces

To make almond curd: Mix gelatin with sugar. Add boiling water and stir until completely dissolved. Cool for 10 minutes. Add milk and extract; stir well. Chill until firmly set. Cut into desired shapes of 3/4 to 1 inch size.

To make syrup: Bring water and sugar to a boil. Stir in almond powder mixture and extract. Chill until very cold.

To serve: Spoon almond curd into individual serving dishes, top with some orange, stir syrup then pour over. Garnish each dish with a bit of red cherry, if red cherries are available. Makes a refreshing dessert.

SWEET DOW SAH GOK
makes 24 sweet crescents

Basic Sweet Dough:

    10 tablespoons (approximately) water

     6 tablespoons firmly packed brown sugar

     2 cups glutinous rice flour (sweet rice
        flour)

    glutinous rice flour for dusting

1 18-oz. can ready-to-use sweetened red bean paste
oil for deep-frying

Bring water and sugar to a boil. Quickly pour
syrup into flour while stirring to get a partially
cooked dough. Knead until smooth, adding more hot
water or flour as needed to make a workable soft
dough. Cover and let rest for 5 minutes.

Lightly dust rolling pin and hands with flour.
Shape dough evenly into two 12" long rolls. Cut
rolls into 24 1-inch pieces. Roll dough, one
piece at a time, into a 3" circle. Place 2 teaspoons filling in center. Fold circle in half
over filling to form a half moon. Tightly seal
and crimp edges. Cover with cloth.

Deep-fry crescents, a few at a time, over medium-
low heat (about 325° F.) to an even golden brown,

about 3 minutes, turning frequently with chopsticks.
Remove with slotted spoon and drain on absorbent
paper. Deep-fried pastries can be refrigerated or
frozen. Place in warm oven to reheat until soft.
See GENERAL HINTS ON DEEP-FRYING.

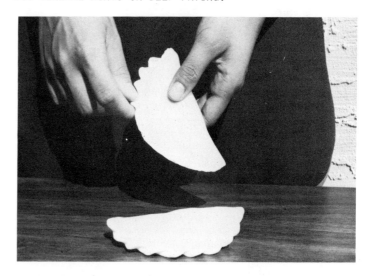

Crimp edges (optional) by holding sealed crescent between thumb and fingers of one hand, with rounded edge
up. Using sides of thumb and forefinger of other hand,
pinch dough along edge of crescent, fluting it as you
would pie crust.

1 recipe Basic Sweet Dough, see page 180

oil for deep-frying

white sesame seeds

Filling: 1 18-oz. can sweetened red bean paste
OR mix together

1 cup crushed dry-roasted peanuts

1/2 cup finely chopped candied citron

1/4 cup chopped glacé red cherries

1 tablespoon softened butter

2 tablespoons corn syrup

Prepare dough as directed. Flour hands. Break off 2 tablespoons of dough and roll it into a ball. Starting from the center, shape dough into a "barrel" about the size of an extra-large egg. Fill the "barrel" two-thirds full with 1 tablespoon filling. Gather the edges, pinching and twisting, thus forming a "vase" with a narrow neck. Twist off the extra dough at the neck and return it to bowl to be used again. Roll the filled dough into a smooth ball with palms of hands. Lightly moisten surface of ball with wet fingers and roll it in sesame seeds. Cover with cloth. Repeat with remaining dough.

Deep-fry gin doy, a few at a time, in 325° F. oil until evenly golden brown, about 6 minutes, constantly turning and rolling with chopsticks. Remove with slotted spoon and drain on absorbent paper. Deep-fried pastries can be refrigerated or frozen. Reheat in warm oven until soft. See GENERAL HINTS ON DEEP-FRYING. Also, see photo on page 16.

Chinese celebrate the arrival of their newborn by giving the baby a party one month after birth. Gin doy and sweet buns (called *sou ho*) are usually served on these occasions.

PUFFED RICE SNACKS
makes 30 pieces

1/2   cup sugar

2   tablespoons butter

1/4   cup water

1/4   cup light corn syrup

1/2   cup roasted peanut halves, chopped walnuts
      or pecans

7-1/2   cups rice krispies cereal or puffed rice

Lightly butter a 13"x9"x2" pan and a knife. Keep
warm, not hot, in oven. Combine sugar, butter, water
and corn syrup in a large pot. Cook, starting with
medium-high heat and gradually reduce heat as syrup
thickens, stirring constantly until syrup has reached
the firm-ball stage (246° F.). Turn off heat. Add
nuts and rice cereal; stir until well coated. Pour
into pan. Spread mixture evenly and press firmly.
Immediately, cut lengthwise into 5 strips, then cut
strips diagonally (or crosswise) into 6 equal parts.
Cool; store in an airtight container.

Deftness is an important factor; work swiftly to
get the best result. Spanish peanut halves are
best. Coarsely crush other varieties. Big chunks
of nuts can cause a complete failure.

Traditionally, some children present this puffed rice
to their godparents as gift on the 9th of September.
It was quite a task for the Chinese villagers to make
this sweet treat. Glutinous rice is steamed, dried,
puffed in cleaned white sand and sieved. Our modern
convenient cereals eliminate all those necessary and
lengthy preparations.

MINI SPONGE CAKES
makes 3 cakes

1 cup sifted cake flour

1 teaspoon baking powder

1/8 teaspoon salt

1/2 cup shortening, at room temperature

1/2 cup sugar

2 large eggs, at room temperature

1 teaspoon almond extract

1/4 cup milk

Grease and lightly flour 3 "flower" shaped baking pans (available at Oriental hardware stores).

Combine flour, baking powder and salt. Set aside. Powder sugar in blender at high speed, about 2 minutes; use the convenient blend-and-store jar. In large mixer bowl, cream powdered sugar and shortening for 1-1/2 minutes. Add eggs and continue creaming until the mixture resembles whipped cream, light and fluffy. Scrape bowl and beaters frequently. Stir in extract. On lowest speed, blend in dry ingredients alternately with milk, adding flour mixture first. Pour batter into prepared pans. Bake in preheated 325° F. oven until wooden pick inserted in center comes out clean, 23 to 25 minutes. See photo on page 16.

STEAMED HONEY SPONGE CAKE
8-10 servings

1 cup sifted cake flour

1 teaspoon baking powder

1/4 teaspoon salt

3 extra-large eggs, separated (at room temperature)

3/4 cup sugar

1 tablespoon honey

1 teaspoon almond extract

1/4 cup water

Combine flour, baking powder and salt; set aside. In a small mixer bowl, beat egg whites until soft peaks form. Gradually add about one-third of the sugar and continue beating until stiff peaks will hold. In large mixer bowl, beat yolks. Gradually add remaining sugar and honey and beat until thick and lemon colored. Stir in extract. Scrape bowl with rubber spatula whenever necessary. On lowest speed, blend the dry ingredients into yolk mixture alternately with water, adding flour mixture first. By hand, gently and evenly fold egg whites into the batter. Pour batter into ungreased 9" tube pan. (Do not use non-stick pans.) Steam over gently boiling water for 20 minutes. Invert pan on bottle or funnel to cool.

FILLINGS

CHILI-FLAVORED PORK FILLING

1/2 lb. lean pork butt, minced, mixed with:

    1/8   teaspoon salt

    2   teaspoons cornstarch

    1   teaspoon sherry

    1/4   to 1/2 teaspoon finely minced
         peeled fresh ginger

Thickener: mix

    1/2   tablespoon cornstarch

    4   tablespoons chicken broth, more
         if needed

oil for cooking

3/4 teaspoon Chinese chili powder, more or less,
depending on spiciness of powder and personal preference

1/2 teaspoon sesame oil

1   to 2 tablespoons minced green onion

2   tablespoons oyster sauce

Dribble 2 to 3 teaspoons oil around sides of very hot wok; swirl to coat wok. Add meat and chili powder; stir-fry until pork is cooked through. Pour in thickener. Stir and cook until translucent. Mix in sesame oil, green onion and oyster sauce. Add 1 to 2 more tablespoons of chicken broth to make a moist filling if mixture is too thick. Cool.

ROASTED PORK FILLING

1/2 lb. char shiu (see CANTONESE ROASTED PORK),
homemade or store-bought, diced to size of petite peas

1/2 teaspoon sesame oil

1   tablespoon oyster sauce

2   to 3 teaspoons Chinese barbecue sauce (some
are thick, some are thinner, depending on the brand)

1   to 2 tablespoons chopped green onion or fresh
coriander

pinch ground pepper

oil for cooking

Thickener: mix

    1-1/2 tablespoons cornstarch

    3/4 cup water

Heat wok until hot. Dribble in 2 to 3 teaspoons of oil around sides of wok; swirl around to coat wok. Pour in thickener; stir and cook until bubbly. Add meat, sesame oil, oyster sauce, barbecue sauce, green onion and ground pepper. Mix well and set aside to cool.

Use filling to stuff buns, pastries, biscuits and other deep-fried or baked dumplings.

PORK AND SHRIMP FILLING

1   tablespoon oil for stir-frying

1   green onion, minced by cutting very finely

Marinate together:

     1/4 lb. medium-sized fresh prawns, shelled, deveined, diced

     1/2 lb. lean pork butt, minced

     1/4 teaspoon salt

       2 teaspoons cornstarch

       1 slice ginger, well minced

       2 teaspoons dark soy sauce

     dash of ground pepper

Mix:

       2 teaspoons cornstarch

       1 tablespoon oyster sauce

     1/4 cup chicken broth

Heat wok. Add oil. When oil is hot, add meat; quickly stir and turn with spatula or chopsticks to break up the lumps and cook through, 3 to 4 minutes. Add cornstarch mixture; stir until thickened. Add onion; mix. Set aside to cool. For raw filling: Mix together diced prawns, minced pork, salt, 1 tablespoon cornstarch, pepper, minced ginger, soy sauce, 1 tablespoon oyster sauce and minced green onion. Omit thickener.

TURKEY WITH DRIED SHRIMP FILLING

Mix together:

       1 lb. ground turkey (or minced lean pork)

     1/4 cup dried shrimp, soaked, picked over, minced

     1/4 to 1/3 cup minced canned mushrooms (dried Chinese mushrooms may be substituted)

     1/2 cup minced water chestnuts

       1 green onion, minced (or equal amount of Chinese chives)

       1 slice peeled ginger, finely minced

       2 tablespoons cornstarch

       a pinch of ground white pepper

     1/2 teaspoon salt

       1 teaspoon *each* sherry, cooking oil, sesame oil and thin soy sauce

       1 tablespoon oyster sauce

This raw mixture makes an excellent filling for many dim sum dumplings.

Or, place mixture in a 10" pyrex pie plate. Steam above boiling water until done, about 15 minutes. Serve with hot cooked rice.

CHILI-FLAVORED BEEF FILLING

Mix together:

- 1 lb. lean ground beef, such as ground round or ground chuck
- 1 slice peeled ginger, well minced
- 1/2 to 1 teaspoon Chinese chili powder, more or less to taste
- 1/2 teaspoon salt
- 4 teaspoons cornstarch
- 1 teaspoon *each* sesame oil and dark soy sauce
- 2 to 3 tablespoons minced green onion or Chinese chives
- 1 tablespoon oyster sauce

Use mixture as raw filling. Or, stir-fry the mixture in 1-1/2 to 2 tablespoons oil for cooked filling.

CURRIED TURKEY FILLING

Mix together:

- 1 lb. ground turkey, thawed and drained if frozen
- 10 canned water chestnuts, minced
- 1 slice peeled ginger, finely minced
- 1 green onion (or equal amount of Chinese chives), minced by cutting finely
- 2 tablespoons cornstarch
- 1 tablespoon curry powder (may be omitted for a different flavor)
- 1/2 teaspoon salt
- 1 teaspoon *each* sherry, cooking oil and sesame oil
- 2 tablespoons oyster sauce

Use this raw mixture to stuff dim sum dumplings.

Or, steam mixture in a 10" pyrex plate and serve it with hot cooked rice. It makes a low-calorie, low-cost, nutritious meat dish.

SAUCES
&
DIPS

A large selection of sauces and dips are available at the Oriental food markets. Take a tour of Chinatown and explore new flavors. Sweet and sour sauce, sweet and sour duck sauce, ready-made extra-hot mustard, hot sauce, chili oil, chili sauce, hot bean sauce, sweet bean sauce, plum sauce and subgum sauce are commonly displayed on the shelves. Find your favorite or create a sauce of your own.

GARLICKY HOISIN DIP

2   teaspoons oil
2   or 3 cloves garlic, finely minced
3   tablespoons hoisin sauce
1   tablespoon water

Heat a small heavy saucepan until hot. Add oil and garlic; stir only to heat through. Mix in hoisin sauce and water.

Serve with dim sum dumplings or meat dishes. Leftovers can be used to marinate meat.

CHILI MUSTARD DIP

1   teaspoon sugar, more or less to taste
2   tablespoons prepared extra-hot Chinese mustard
1   tablespoon dark soy sauce
1/2   tablespoon rice vinegar
1/2   teaspoon chili oil, more or less to taste
      and only if desired

Stir together sugar, mustard, soy sauce and rice vinegar to blend. Add chili oil, if needed, and stir again. Serve with dim sum dumplings.

SWEET AND SOUR SAUCE

2 teaspoons oil
2 (for thin sauce) or 3 (for thicker sauce) teaspoons cornstarch
1/8 teaspoon salt
2 tablespoons *each* brown sugar (firmly packed), white vinegar and catsup
1/2 cup water

Heat a small heavy-bottomed saucepan until hot. Add oil. When oil is hot, pour in mixture of remaining ingredients; stir until thickened and bubbly.

Use for dipping sauce or as sweet and sour sauce for certain dishes.

This sweet and sour sauce has the sharp strong flavor of white vinegar, yet is sweet and tempting.

SPICED SALT

Mix as much as needed in the following ratio:
3 tablespoons salt
2 teaspoons Szechwan peppercorns

Toast the mixture in a heavy, dry, and ungreased pan over low heat until peppercorns are slightly brown and fragrant, about 5 minutes, stirring frequently. Cool. Grind mixture to a powder in the blender. Sift through a fine sieve. Store powder in a clean dry jar. Use on fried or roasted meat.

CHILI OIL

1/4 to 1/3 cup salad oil
2 or 3 dried red hot chili peppers, depending on personal preference

Heat oil until very hot but not smoking; add chili peppers and fry for a minute or two. Remove from heat. Leave peppers in oil until the desired flavor is obtained.

All garnishes can be prepared at leisure and refrigerated in plastic container for one week or longer, depending on the vegetable. Garnishes made out of hard vegetables such as carrots will keep for a month. A beautifully decorated dish is vividly alive and reflects one's artistic talent. Other decorative garnishes, including carrot wheels, onion flowers, tomato bowls, cucumber roses, and a beautiful three dimensional butterfly are presented in Lonnie Mock's *FAVORITE DIM SUM* cookbook, pages 111 through 115.

PEPPER FAN

Cut a wedge off a green or red bell pepper. Cut wedge in half. Then cut half-wedge into several "petals" without cutting through the narrow end.

COILED ROSE

Peel a continuous strip around a tomato (orange or lemon). Loosely wind strip to resemble a rose.

ZIG ZAG LEMON

Cut the top third off. Make "V" cuts around the cut edge.

RADISH PETALS

Put a radish between two chopsticks. Slice radish as thinly as possible. Chopsticks will prevent knife slicing through. Soak in ice water. Petals will spread open.

FRUIT BASKET

Mentally mark a small strip across the center top
of an orange (lemon, cantaloupe, tomato or water-
melon). This center strip will become the handle.
Cut off a wedge on both sides of handle as shown
on left of photo. Scoop out pulp, thus creating
a hollow basket. Fill basket with other small
garnishes, fruits, or coriander. Large melon
baskets can be used to hold melon balls and other
fruits. Very attractive!

ONION BRUSH

Use only the bulb portion of green onion. Cut a
stalk 3" to 4" in length. Cut both ends into fine
shreds without cutting through the "waist" in the
middle. Soak in ice water and refrigerate until
split ends spring out into fringes. Use for garnish
or serve with CRISP AND SAVORY PEKING DUCK, see
recipe.

FLOWER WHEEL

Cut a slice of turnip, then cut notches all around
to resemble petals as shown. Similarly cut a slice
of carrot and cut an indention in the middle.
Center carrot slice over turnip flower and place
a pea in the indention.

CARROT BRUSH

Cut a 2" section from the large end (or middle) of
a carrot. Trim to resemble a frustum. Place frustum,
large end up, on table. Cut into shreds two-thirds
way down in checker board fashion. Gently spread
"bristles" and soak in ice water overnight. Carrot
brush keeps for weeks in plastic container under
refrigeration.

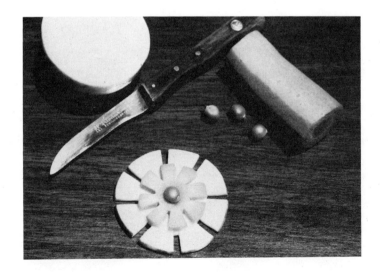

CARROT BUTTERFLY

Peel carrot; discard this brownish covering. Peel
long strips with potato peeler. Individually wind
2 strips and place together in opposite directions
as shown. Pretty and easy.

TOMATO BUTTERFLY

Select a very firm tomato with green shoulders. (Red
and green make a beautiful contrast.) Cut a half
slice as shown on upper left. Next trim off two "V"
notches as indicated on upper right. Similarly cut
a second half slice. Put slices together in opposite
directions to form a butterfly.

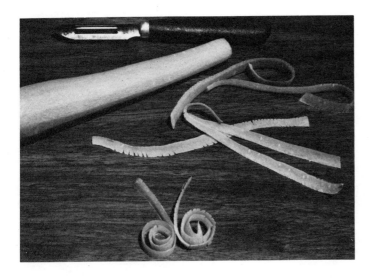

CUCUMBER OR ZUCCHINI FAN

PEPPER ORCHID

Cut a 2" section off the stem end. Cut section in half lengthwise. Cut this, in turn, into very thin slices without cutting through to the stem end. Bend and curve every other slice back toward stem end to form a loop.

Select a firm yellow, orange or red chili. Carefully cut pepper into 5 or 6 petals. Do not remove seeds and pulp; save for stamens. Soak in ice water overnight. Petals will spring out and will eventually curl. It makes a beautiful decoration.

MENUS

Below are eight suggested menus, designed to suit even the most sophisticated palate. Advance preparations are discussed in individual recipes. Each menu is carefully planned to provide harmony, contrast and variety. The work load is balanced. For example, a lengthy recipe is offset by a simple one, and last-minute cooking is reduced to a minimum. Cooking methods in each menu utilize the steamer, the skillet, the deep-fryer, the wok and/or the oven so that even if you decide to cook the entire meal at the last minute, you won't have to wash and wait for the same pan. Of course, feel free to select and combine recipes to design your own menus. Furthermore, one or two dishes can be integrated into your own cuisine. How about Chinese chicken salad with hamburgers or refreshing Chinese-style soup with spaghetti?

Each menu can serve from four to six persons, depending on the appetite and occasion. The Chinese custom of dining consists of at least a few dishes at a meal. The number of servings indicated in the recipes is predicated on this concept. Exercise your own judgment. If it is essential to double the quantity of any stir-fry recipe, it is better to repeat the cooking process. Do not stir-fry twice the amount all at one time. For a party of two, two dishes are usually sufficient.

Since rice is the bulk of a meal, steamed rice appears in every dinner menu. Occasionally, fried rice or a noodle dish may be substituted. In China, rice is regarded as a life food. When dinner is served, one says, "Come eat rice." Upon meeting a friend, one greets, "Have you had rice yet?"

Beverage choices may be tea, sparkling cider, 7-UP or light wine. For a family-style dinner, soup is consumed intermittently throughout the meal.

MENU #1: Dim Sum Luncheon

        FRIED FUN GOR or STUFFED BONELESS DRUMSTICKS
        SILVER-THREAD SAUSAGE ROLLS
        RICE MEAT BALLS
        CHICKEN SALAD WITH GARLIC-SOY DRESSING or GINGER SALAD
        SESAME COOKIES
        tea

MENU #2: Dim Sum Luncheon

        CHINESE SPRING ROLLS or DEEP-FRIED HAR KOW or SANDWICH POCKETS
        COILED SAUSAGE BUNS
        WON TON WAR MEIN or BEEF LO MEIN WITH VEGETABLES
        CRUNCHY SESAME BOW TIES
        tea

MENU #3: Family Dinner I

        CRISP AROMATIC FISH or BRAISED SOY DUCK
        CHICKEN CORN SOUP or SEAWEED TOFU SOUP
        CHAR SHIU FRIED RICE
        dessert of your choice
        beverage

MENU #4: Family Dinner II

        STEAMED FISH or STEAMED PRAWNS IN BLACK BEAN SAUCE
        CRUNCHY TENDER CHICKEN or DRUMSTICKS SIMMERED IN GARLIC SAUCE
        STIR-FRIED OYSTER BEEF WITH ONION
        dessert of your choice
        rice
        beverage

MENU #5: Family Dinner III

       SIMPLE-N-GOOD ROASTED CHICKEN or FLAVOR-POTTED CHICKEN
       TOMATO BEEF or BEEF FRIDAY CURRY or STEAMED BEEF
       CAULIFLOWER IN HAM SAUCE or FIVE-FLAVORED CABBAGE STIR FRY
       dessert of your choice
       rice
       beverage

MENU #6: Spicier Dinner

       POULTRY STUFFING or SHREDDED CHICKEN WITH GARLIC SAUCE
       MONGOLIAN LAMB or MONGOLIAN BEEF
       POACHED FISH
       SESAME-PEANUT SOUP for dessert or REFRESHING VEGETABLE SOUP to accompany meal
       rice
       beverage

MENU #7: Elegant Company Dinner I

       STIR-FRIED FISH FILLET or NAPA CABBAGE PEEKS THROUGH CLOUDS
       MELT-IN-THE-MOUTH STEAKS
       PRESSED DUCK or CRISP AND TANGY LEMON CHICKEN
       GINGER COOKIES
       rice
       beverage

MENU #8: Elegant Company Dinner II

       BUTTERFLY PRAWNS for appetizer
       BEEF WITH PLENTY OF VEGGIES or CAULIFLOWER ON CLOUD EARS
       CRISPY AND SAVORY PEKING DUCK (with or without plain steamed buns)
       SWEET AND SOUR PORK or SWEET AND SOUR FISH
       ALMOND CURD
       rice
       beverage

ORDER FORM

NAME_____

NO. AND STREET_____

CITY_____

ADDRESS ALL INQUIRIES & BOOK ORDERS

STATE_____

ZIP_____

to

ALPHA GAMMA ARTS
P. O. BOX 4671
WALNUT CREEK, CALIFORNIA 94596-0671

description	quantity	unit price	postage & handling*	total
FAVORITE DIM SUM		$4.95		
141 AND ONE-HALF CHINESE-STYLE CHICKEN RECIPES		$5.95		
EXCEL IN CHINESE COOKING		$7.95		

* For orders of 1 to 10 books, the rate is $1 for the first book. Add 40¢ per book up to 10 books. For larger orders, please write to us.

FAVORITE DIM SUM

Dim sum is a special aspect of the Chinese cuisine. Dim sum foods can be sweet, sour or salty. Dishes can be served as hors d'oeuvres, light supper, lunch, brunch, midnight snacks, breakfast or whenever the heart craves a tempting morsel.

Favorite Dim Sum presents the newest shapes and ideas in dim sum making, featuring more than 100 choice recipes, fancy garnishes, suggested menus, sauces and dips, additional filling recipes and tea.

Recipes include all the popular dim sum dishes such as char shiu bao, pot stickers, mo shu pork, Mandarin pancakes, sizzling rice soup, har gow, rice noodle rolls, fun gor, custard tarts, taro turnovers, flaky char shiu so, thousand layer bread, stuffed prawns, crisp ginger beef rolls, Chinese sausage pancakes, shrimp rolls, chow mein and much more.

Each suggested menu is carefully selected from recipes prepared by different cooking techniques. For example: One dish is pan-fried, one steamed, one baked, so that your dishes aren't delayed and overcooked, and your meal is ready all at once even if you decide to cook the entire meal at the last minute.

Favorite Dim Sum is written in the American language, fully illustrated with instructional photos and step-by-step sketches. Information on deep-frying, stir-frying, steaming, pan-frying and ingredients is given in detail.

More and more Americans are discovering that dim sum dining is an enjoyable experience. Anyone can learn to make delicious dim sum by following the precise directions and illustrations given in Favorite Dim Sum.

141 AND ONE-HALF CHINESE-STYLE CHICKEN RECIPES

141 AND ONE-HALF CHINESE-STYLE CHICKEN RECIPES is a handsome, complete, 208-page volume, composed of 143 recipes plus variations. There is a recipe to suit every taste bud and any occasion, from elaborate to informal. Recipes cover every aspect of dining: breakfast, brunch, dim sum luncheon, one-dish meals, entrees, elegant banquet specialties, midnight snacks, pre-dinner appetizers and in-between-meal snacks.

Chicken can be stir-fried, roasted, boiled, braised, deep-fried, steamed, poached, smoked, barbecued, and recipes sometimes utilize a combination of two different cooking techniques. Because recipes cover every aspect of dining and are so diversified in cooking methods, one can actually serve a three-course chicken dinner.

Other special features are: cutting up a chicken into parts, deboning chicken breast, skinning a whole fowl, deboning a whole fowl, and chopping a whole fowl into serving pieces and reassembling the pieces into the original form. A convenient Chinese shopping list is provided.

Some specific recipes are: Almond Chicken, Cashew Chicken With Vegetables, Chicken Over Sizzling Rice, Chicken With Asparagus, Chicken With Lemon Sauce, Chinese Chicken Salad, Crispy Chicken, Firepot Dinner, Hot And Sour Soup, Hot And Sour Chicken, Kung Pao Chicken, Mo Shu Chicken, Pineapple Chicken Delight, Roasted Soy Chicken, Roasted Turkey, Steamed Chicken In Black Bean Sauce, Stir-Fried Chicken (5 recipes), Stuffed Boneless Whole Chicken, Stuffed Boneless Chicken Wings, Velvety Chicken, Taro Rounds and others.

Chicken is nutritious, economical, versatile, low in cholesterol, low in fat, high in protein, but best of all, d-e-l-i-c-i-o-u-s!